001.64
GRE

W9-AUP-518

DATE DUE			
Josh August 31, 1993			

001.64
GRE

Greenblatt, Stanley.

Understand computers
through common
sense.

HOMESTEAD HIGH SCHOOL
LIBRARY MEDIA CENTER

428320 #6564   02131C

001.64
GRE
6564

$6.95

10/08/84

Follett Co.

Understand
Computers
Through
Common Sense

Stanley Greenblatt

CORNERSTONE LIBRARY
Published by Simon & Schuster
NEW YORK

Copyright © 1979, 1983 by Stanley Greenblatt
All rights reserved
including the right of reproduction
in whole or in part in any form
Published by Cornerstone Library,
A Simon & Schuster Division of Gulf & Western Corporation
Simon & Schuster Building
1230 Avenue of the Americas
New York, New York 10020
CORNERSTONE LIBRARY and colophon are trademarks of
Simon & Schuster, registered in the U.S Patent and Trademark
Office.

10 9 8 7 6 5 4 3 2 1

Manufactured in the United States of America

ISBN 0-346-12529-4

To my parents
JENNIE GREENBLATT
HYMAN GREENBLATT

CONTENTS

1

Introduction

Just a few years ago, most computer users were highly trained technical individuals who confined their applications to the business and/or scientific communities. But with the advent of smaller, less expensive computers combined with entertainment applications such as home video games, the computer is now within the reach of the layperson. In fact, personal computers are sweeping the country. While they were originally purchased by many in order to bring the "penny arcade" into their living rooms, these personal and hobby computers have also resulted in bringing new technology to the user's fingertips. So whether your interest is in the large-scale "number cruncher" or the small "computer in your pocket," welcome to the information world.

Did you ever want to blame your car when the traffic cop pulled you over for speeding? Though you may have been tempted to, you also knew it wouldn't work. You were the driver, you failed to obey the speed limit, you were the culprit. No judge would accept a plea of not guilty under the circumstances.

Surprisingly, if you were operating a computer instead

of an automobile, you stand a good chance of blaming the machine and getting away with it. The newspapers are full of stories about so-called computer errors, ranging from the amusing anecdotes of the collection agency who dunned its client for the ten cents owed to the more serious problems such as the two great New York blackouts.

Why is the automobile's driver responsible for the traffic violation, but the "computer" is the culprit in the big blackouts? One of the major reasons is that we all understand the relation between driver and automobile, while we tend to think of the computer as a mysterious product operated by contemporary equivalents of highly technological witch doctors. In the case of the computer, ignorance breeds fear and confusion rather than bliss. As a result, we tend to accept the computer's quirks more readily than we accept the weather. After all, most people don't complain about the computerman nearly as much as they do about the weatherman.

It can't be emphasized too often and too strongly that the computer is just another machine. And, as with all machines, the computer was invented by humans to be used by humans and to be understood by humans. There's nothing mysterious about computers. They're wonderful machines for performing certain tasks. On the other hand, your daughter wouldn't want to marry one (although she certainly wouldn't go wrong with a solid computer professional).

Stop and think of all the fairly advanced technological gadgets that you deal with each day. While you may not have any idea of how the telephone or television works, you use them everyday. Indeed, you are quite capable of buying a television set that meets your requirements as to price, screen size, color, and all the other factors that go into the decision. The telephone company offers many options with its service; unlimited calling, dial or touchtone, a variety of extensions and colors. Yet, you are not overwhelmed when selecting a telephone.

Photographs obtained courtesy of Digital Equipment Corporation.

1. Computer System (keyboard printer, CRT terminal, magnetic tape drives, central processor, line printer, disk drives)

Although you may know nothing about communications signals and electrons, you do know when you are getting good value for your television and telephone dollars. The average citizen does not require a telephone genius to tell him if his telephone is working properly. You know almost immediately if there's excessive noise on the telephone line, if wayward signals caused a wrong number, or if your conversation was suddenly disconnected. And when you call the business office, they don't tell you "there's a problem with the computer." You wouldn't accept such a lame explanation. Well, you shouldn't be required to accept less when it comes to computers.

Throughout this book, we want to demonstrate the simplicity of the computer so that you can gain an understanding of this important machine. You'll discover that you are already familiar with many machines that are in many respects more complicated than computers. While a high fidelity system is common to most households, in many respects it is more expensive and difficult to manufacture and operate to its fullest performance capabilities than is a computer. But you probably own some form of high fidelity equipment; perhaps an inexpensive phonograph, or a more elaborate setup with am/fm radio, microphone for recordig, several speakers, and any of the various exotic optional components available in today's marketplace.

While you probably don't care about the magnetic layer on the tape recording system or the superhetrodyne oscillator of the tuner, you are perfectly capable of knowing when a hi-fi system is producing good sound. You don't need an advanced degree to shop around for a system that fits your pocketbook and desires. You have no problem understanding what special features such as microphones, stereophonic sound, and automatic turntables provide. Believe it or not, you can understand the computer just as well as you do a hi-fi system without

FIGURE 1.1   BASIC HIFI/COMPUTER SYSTEM ANALOGY DIAGRAM

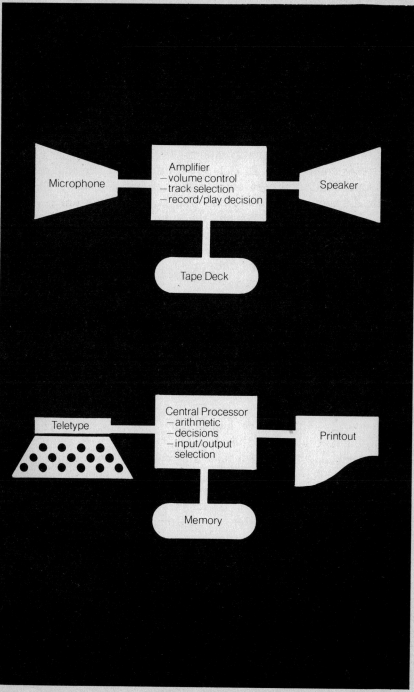

getting bogged down into the nitty gritty of logic circuits and other technological detail.

Computers and hi-fi systems are surprisingly analogous, not only in configuration (as seen in Figure 1.1) but also, especially for personal computers, from the selling aspect as well. Stop by Loonie Louis's Discount House of Audio Stereo or Ruth Janet's Platter Palace and you will see almost as many models of personal computers available for purchase as stereo components. In fact, you'll find that many of the personal computers cost less than the stereo systems.

Both systems can record and play back information. In the case of the hi-fi system, the information is usually music, but it can be a Shakespearian play or a presidential news conference. Computer information is usually more mundane, perhaps a report on a parts inventory or the weekly payroll.

In comparing the two systems then, they both require some device for entering information, a way of storing the information, a procedure for playing back the information, and a device on which the information is played back. While this may appear to be complicated, consider how simply it's done for the hi-fi.

The microphone provides the mechanism for entering information. You talk or sing into the microphone and the sound is captured on a magnetic tape or cassette. We could have said that the sound is "stored" instead of captured. A phonograph record also stores information. Generally, a record producer arranges for a symphonic orchestra or popular singer to record in a studio. The music is captured on the disk (or even on an 8-track tape) and sold over the counter to consumers.

Playback on the hi-fi system is accomplished through the speaker. Another important component of the hi-fi system is the amplifier and its associated dials for changing volume, selecting whether the system should be recording or playing, and even whether the tape deck, phonograph, or radio should be involved. While a human

being usually must physically set the appropriate amplifier selection knobs, some automatic features are also
available. For example, some systems have an automatic
volume control which prevents the volume from becoming higher or lower than wanted. While this control is not
achieved in quite the same way that a computer program
instructs its system, the automatic volume feature
provides a predetermined control capability; the user
selects a volume and by setting the feature designates that
whenever the volume changes the system will automatically make a proper adjustment.

A computer has components just like the hi-fi. When
all the components are put together, it's called a computer system.

Computers can also function like a hi-fi by accepting
information from a microphone and playing back recorded
messages. In a sense, the computer controls an electronic
post office where "letters" are recorded voice messages. The
"envelopes" with the sender's and receiver's addresses are
supplied with the messages in electronic form. Other forms
of electronic mail utilize written messages. This type of
computer usage is becoming more prevalent and represents
one of the applications sometimes known as the "electronic
office."

Usually, a special form of typewriter is wired into the so-
called central processor in a similar fashion to how the hi-fi's
microphone is wired into the amplifier. Using the typewriter
to enter information (or also teletype machines) a human
being can now communicate. The human types information
using the keyboard while the typewriter converts the characters to electrical signals understood by the central processor.
In essence the computer is participating in a sophisticated
type of Morse code.

To reiterate, the typewriter serves the same function as
a microphone. For getting information out of the computer, most systems use some form of printer. In reverse to
the typewriter keyboard input, the computer signals are

converted into characters that make sense to a human being when read from a printed page. Computers are storage systems quite similar to hi-fi systems; magnetic tapes; magnetic cassettes, and devices that look and act like phonograph records. Computer people call these storage units "memory." Although in Figure 1, the memory is shown outside the central processor, it can be an integral part, just as the tape deck in a hi-fi system can be built into the amplifier console.

The central processor is the component within a computer system that controls all activity. All input, output, and memory devices attach to the central processor. The central processor is completely automatic and can operate independent of human intervention. The human loads the central processor with instructions and the "program" makes all decisions, performs all arithmetic, and makes all input/output device selections. But don't get the impression that the central processor is magical. Before it can perform, the human was required to provide proper instructions and to plan for every contingency. We'll see in later chapters that the central processor is only as good as the human beings who give it its initial instructions.

The remaining chapters will discuss each major computer system component and show how a complete system operates.

Programming explains the general nature of computer instructions. The chapter introduces a limited set of instructions to demonstrate in plain English how computer people think when preparing computer instructions. We don't intend to make you a programmer, but do want to give you a solid feel of the disciplined thinking required for computer programming. Another major point we want to get across is why so-called computer errors are really human errors.

Central Processor explains the importance of this component and how it relates to the system as a whole.

We'll discuss the variety of optional features offered, some aspects of its construction, and where such terms as computer generations and minicomputers come from.

Memory will take you through the various types of storage media such as cassettes, disks, core, and semiconductor. You'll see how to determine which types of memories to use for different jobs and why cost is an important factor. The chapter will also discuss a rule of thumb procedure to figure out how much information can be stored by different size memories.

Typing In/Printing Out is basically how the human communicates with a computer system. A variety of devices are available for getting information into and out of computer for human reading and understanding. As with memories, there are trade offs between how well the devices perform and their cost.

Putting It All Together presents an overview of a complete system's operation. We'll discuss how operating systems and compilers work, and tell something about batch, real time, and time sharing processing.

Crime and Personal Computer Controls discusses the nature of controls in assuring authorized and accurate use of computer resources, and approaches for instituting such controls in input, software, and output areas with special emphasis on how these apply to personal and hobby computers.

Index is an alphabetical listing of some of the more significant computer terms and jargon words. Frequently, computer people (like other technologists) speak in a unique language. The lay person is usually baffled by these highly specialized terms. However, the concepts are not very difficult. In an attempt to bridge the communication gap between those knowledgeable with computers and those who are not, each term is given with appropriate reference to its description in the text.

2

Programming

You don't have to be a doctor to know you are sick. Similarly, you can think in computer terms and understand what the computer is instructed to do without being a computer programmer.

In the following, we will discuss the general nature of computer instructions and demonstrate some examples of the disciplined thinking required for computer programming. You'll also find that in many of your daily experiences, you are probably already thinking in computer compatible terms, but haven't realized it.

Hardware/Software

Perhaps one of the most confusing pieces of computer terminology is the difference between "hardware" and "software." Actually, the distinctions are quite simple.

Hardware is the term used to denote the physical

equipment while software denotes the written set of instructions. Although the hardware/software distinction is popular among computer people and their technological colleagues, there are many other examples of the hardware/software differences.

Consider a musical piece played on a piano. The piano is made of wood and metal, and is heavy and hard. A composer writes instructions (called musical notes) intended to direct the pianist. In this case the piano comes under the category of hardware, while the set of instructions comes under software. It may appear silly, but because instructions are usually written on paper for heavy machines and devices, they're called "software." Table 2.1 shows a variety of hardware/software combinations that you meet in your daily life.

A piano concerto is like a three legged stool; if any single leg is weak the stool will collapse.

One leg is the quality of the instrument. The piano must be in tune and have a good sound. Even the uninitiated can notice the difference bettween a cheap, poorly made piano, and a concert grand piano made by one of the well-known manufacturers.

The musical notes themselves provide the second leg of the stool. A Mozart concerto or a Cole Porter tune contains delicate refrains and a variety of brilliant musical stanzas. History has forgotten the names of the many composers who wrote bad music. We might say these were bad programmers. Good music can range from the highly technical classical piece to the simple popular tune. Similarly, a computer program can range in application from calculating the weekly pyroll to the more romantic and probably more interesting pastime of computer dating.

The third leg in the stool is the pianist or operator. A bad piano player sitting at a great piano while playing a great concerto will produce a bad concert. Of course, all pianists don't have to be great in order to produce a good

TABLE 2.1

Examples of Hardware/Software Combinations In Everyday Life

ACTIVITY: PIANO PLAYING
Hardware: piano
Software: notes on music sheet

ACTIVITY: TELEPHONE CALL
Hardware: the telephone
Software: telephone directory

ACTIVITY: COOKING
Hardware: pots, pans, ingredients
Software: recipe listing ingredients and giving cooking instructions

ACTIVITY: FOOTBALL
Hardware: equipment, ball, field
Software: set of plays; special coaching and signals

ACTIVITY: DRIVING A CAR
Hardware: automobile
Software: roadmap

ACTIVITY: MODEL AIRPLANE BUILDING
Hardware: balsa wood, glue, rubber bands
Software: design plans

show, nor must all instruments or compositions be classics. The piano concert is a system comprised of three parts that join together to produce a total effect. As a member of the audience, you will either be pleased with the final result, displeased, or perhaps remain indifferent. Whether or not you return to hear another concert will depend on the total impact.

The computer system is very similar to the concert. The operator, the hardware, and the software must all work together to provide a total system capability.

A Computer Can Be Too Obedient

A computer can be among the most obedient and faithful servants available. However, because a computer is completely lacking in initiative, it must receive all directions from its human supervisor. As a result, proper communications between the human and computer is extremely important. As an example, reflect on the times you said something to a friend or business associate only to discover later that you were totally misunderstood. There's an old cliche that goes "I didn't hear what you thought you were saying."

When a fellow human misunderstands what you mean, serious problems can develop, but these problems are limited to isolated instances and the confusion is usually clarified before much damage is done. Also, a human can usually apply enough intelligent reasoning to decide that what was conveyed cannot possibly be what was meant. When a computer misunderstands what you meant, however, the consequences can be great and in some cases disastrous.

Why do we stress this difference? Because it's important to bear in mind that while computers can perform calculations and other logical instructions much faster than humans, computers cannot think.

When you are asked to do something that seems peculiar, you probably ask the person who has asked you to do the thing to clarify the instruction. Your response is commonly called "feedback." You have let the person know that his directive was unclear or improper. He then has the opportunity to reconsider his request and make appropriate corrections.

Imagine for a moment that you had a servant who blindly obeyed your every utterance. He would not stop to consider whether or not you truly meant every word you said. For example, there are times when you may be exasperated and tell someone to "go jump in the lake." You really don't expect the order to be obeyed. While this may be a trivial example, history is filled with many cases in which blind obedience led to great tragedy. The Light Brigade gallantly charged with cannons to the right and cannons to the left. If the commanders at headquarters had received "feedback" from the men of the Light Brigade they probably would have rescinded the order to charge.

In many cases, a computer follows a similar path to that of the Light Brigade. Some people may be surprised at this statement. We tend to think of the computer as the highest form of logic machine. Indeed, the computer does operate on a strictly logical basis. However, many directives can be totally logical and at the same time completely lacking in sense. A friend can "jump in the lake," soldiers can gallantly charge to their self destruction; these are both physically possible actions, but are they sensible?

When you're in a hurry to arrive at a particular destination, an automobile will get you there faster than if you walk. On the other hand, if you start out in the wrong direction, the faster automobile will get you more lost than if you walked. For example, after walking an hour you may go one or two miles in the wrong direction, but an automobile going at fifty miles an hour will take you fifty miles out of your way. Then, if the automobile runs out of gas, you must walk fifty miles to get where you wanted to be in the first place. Instead of saving you time, the automobile's speed in this case has caused you considerable problems.

Just as with an automobile, the computer's operating speed can be a positive time saver, but if misdirected can cause considerably more problems than a slower human could.

As an example, consider the difference between checks manually prepared by humans and those generated by computers. During the time it takes for a human to prepare one check, a computer can print hundreds. If each check has an error of ten dollars, the manually prepared checks may be in error by perhaps a hundred dollars after only an hour's worth of check preparation. The computer on the other hand may be in error by many thousands of dollars.

Actually, each example of "computer error" mentioned here was really an example of faulty programming caused by human error. We did not intend through this example to knock the computer; it's a great piece of technology. Our intention was to stress the inherent dangers that can arise if you expect the computer to do your thinking for you.

Consider All Possibilities

Almost everyone is familiar with Paul Revere's ride to warn the American colonists of the British troop's arrival. According to Longfellow's poem *The Midnight Ride of Paul Revere*, Revere instructed the men at the lookout on

the Old North Church "one if by land, two if by sea." In a
very real sense, this simple instruction can be considered
one of the first computer programs written for the United
States.

Of course, the computer was invented almost two
hundred years after Paul Revere's ride. Nevertheless, the
art of preparing instructions in advance for predictable
situations has been practiced in all societies way before
computers were invented.

How good was Paul Revere's program? First he considered from which directions the British troops might
come. Since Boston is a port city, it was natural to expect
them to arrive by land or by sea.

The "computer hardware" consisted of the Old North
Church window, two lanterns, and a signalman. Since
contemporary programmers are not as poetic as Henry
Wadsworth Longfellow, today the instructions would be
expressed as follows:

IF the British are coming by land THEN shine one
lantern

IF the British are coming by sea THEN shine two
lanterns

The so-called contingency statement (IF a specified
condition is obeyed THEN take the following action) is a
popular instruction. It's one of the important elements
that enables computers to make choices.

However, the instructions set contained a flaw. For-
tunately for Paul Revere and his comrades in arms the
programming flaw did not become apparent so their
adventure rates a place in history. What if the British had
come by both land and sea? Based on the instructions
already established, it would have been impossible to
convey the information. Since they expected to shine two
lanterns at most, a third lantern was not available. Even if
the third lantern had been available, would the signalman at the church tower have been blindly obedient in
which case he would have done nothing since he had no

specific directive for the both land and sea situation? Or if the signalman did use some initiative and did shine three lanterns, would Revere have understood the signal's meaning and deployed his troops appropriately?

Just from this simple example, it's evident that the programmer must plan for all contingencies. In reality, there's nothing very profound about this statement. You plan for most contingencies in your daily life. However, you probably don't consider yourself to be doing programming.

From Paul Revere's time to today, we're faced with contingency situations that require advanced planning. Various touring agencies provide customers with special strip road maps. They're convenient maps consisting of narrow pages in book form that depict the highway you'll be using in your travels. For example, if you plan to travel from New York to California via Route 66, the strip map will highlight all the cities and towns on that route. The map will also indicate the mileage between all points.

To get proper use from the strip map, you are required to plan your route in advance. If you decide later to travel an alternate route, the strip map will become useless since it concentrates totally on the preplanned route. Therefore, if the road is closed at some point and a detour is required, you may stand a very good chance of getting very lost. Unless you have a contingency plan; a foldout map depicting all United States highways. Indeed, most touring agencies provide customers with both types of maps. Experience has taught them the necessity of contingency planning.

If it's important for humans to plan for contingencies, it's absolutely necessary for programmers to do the same for computers. At least the human can rethink his problem and search for a solution. A computer will simply sit with its lights flashing incapable of making a decision because it did not receive any instructions for the unanticipated contingency.

In fact, most so-called computer errors occur when the computer is confronted with making a decision for which it did not receive instructions. Clearly, this is not the computer's error, the error was committed by the programmer. We emphasize this point because the lay person may have been enchanted by the computer's mystique. In too many cases **the** programmer has not been given sufficient briefing about the problem and he in turn has been unable to provide the computer with all the necessary instructions. All human parties concerned fall into a trap in assuming that the computer will figure out some way to solve the problem. Everyone "passes the buck" to the computer and when something goes wrong, they shout "computer error."

How to Think in Computer Terms

You can understand the thinking required to write computer instructions. It's not necessary to actually learn a computer language. The specific language used to convey the information is not as important as the content of the message itself. Once you have decided the instructions you want performed, you can then find a programmer to translate your English language instructions into a language that the computer can understand.

The process is similar to translating a novel from English to French. The original author expresses his ideas in one language, however the reader is fully capable of understanding the story only after it has been translated into his own language. The translator is the intermediary. If the novel was exciting, romantic, adventurous, etc. in its original language, it will have the same impact if it is properly translated.

The first step in developing a computer program is to break the operation down into basic steps. As an example of the considerations involved, we'll discuss the familiar activity of placing a telephone call.

You're probably so familiar with placing telephone calls that you never stop to think about the many individual decisions and actions you take for completing this activity. The sequence of events is as follows:

A. You know the name of the individual
B. Locate the individual's telephone number
   1. *This operation will be accomplished by looking up the name in a telephone directory or, if none is available, by calling the operator for information. Notice that in this step you have a choice and must make a decision.*
C. Connect the telephone to receive a dial tone
   1. *This operation is usually performed by lifting the receiver. In some cases it can be accomplished automatically by pressing a button or throwing a switch.*
D. Dial the telephone number
   1. *This is a repetitive operation. A local call requires dialing seven numbers (or pushing seven buttons if you are using a Touchtone). The seven numbers must be dialed in a specified sequence. For example 478-1295.*
E. Test for a connection with the party dialed
   1. *After you dial the number, you then listen for a ringing on the other end of the line. If the telephone on the other end is busy, you'll hear a "busy signal."*
   2. *While the other telephone is ringing, you know that a connection was made. But you do not know if the party is at home. So your test continues by allowing the telephone to ring perhaps five or six times. If nobody answers, you hang up.*

3. In the cases of the busy signal or no
   answer, you will try again at a later time. If
   you remember the telephone number, then
   you will repeat the process from step C. If
   you have forgotten the telephone number,
   you will repeat the process from step B.

Each of the actions discussed above can be broken
down further into smaller logical steps. In fact, you can
write a step-by-step procedure that can be followed by
anyone, even someone who has never placed a telephone
call. So that you can keep track of the process, the major
steps will be labelled A through E as in the previous case.

A. You know the name of the individual
B. Locate the individual's telephone number
   1. Look up the individual's name in the
      directory
      a. Did you find the name?
         Yes—go to step C.
         No—do the next instruction
   2. Call the information operator and obtain
      the number
C. Connect the telephone to receive a dial tone
   1. Lift the receiver and place it to your ear
      a. Do you hear a dial tone?
         Yes—go to step D.
         No—go back to the beginning of step
         C.
D. Dial the telephone number 478-1295
   1. Place index finger in hole over the number
      "4"
   2. Move dial until it stops
   3. Remove index finger from dial
   4. Wait for dial to return to starting position
   5. Place index finger in hole over the number
      "7"
   6. Move dial until it stops
   7. Remove index finger from dial

8. Wait for dial to return to starting position (The sequence Place, Move, Remove, Wait will be repeated five more times for the numbers 8,1,2,9,5. In the interest of brevity, we won't repeat the sequence here. Later we'll show you how this can be expressed more concisely as a subroutine. In any case if all the steps were written, the last Remove sequence would be labelled 28 and the next instruction is 29)

29. Go to step E.

E. Test for a connection with the party dialed
1. Do you hear a "busy signal"?
    a. Yes
        •   hang up the receiver
        •   wait five minutes
        •   go back to step B (if you forget the number) or to step C (if you remember the number)
    b. No
        •   go to next step
2. Has the party on the other telephone answered?
    a. Yes
        •   begin your conversation
        •   complete your conversation
        •   hang up the telephone
    b. No
        •   listen for next ring
        •   count the number of rings
        •   is this the fifth ring?
            Yes—go to step E1a
            No—go to step E2b

This example of dialing a telephone call is fairly simple. Each step is easy to understand. The logic from one step to another is also simple and requires no specialized education or training on your part. However, even this simple example requires many steps.

Naturally, more complicated programs contain very many more steps. Again each step is simple, but you can sometimes get lost in the maze of the "go to" instructions that send you hopping all over the place to different steps.

Flowcharts

Just as an architect uses a floor plan to get a picture of a building in the design stage, the computer programmer uses a visual device called the flowchart to "see" the program flow. A flowchart is a roadmap of the program. We speak of program "flow" because for the program to be properly completed the correct instructions must be executed in the correct time sequence. For example, in the previous example, step B (locating the telephone number) must be completed before you can begin step D (dialing the telephone number).

Figure 2.1 is a flowchart of the telephone dialing program. At first glance it may appear to be a complicated maze of boxes and lines. However, it's nothing more than a map of the program and once you become familiar with flowchart you will discover how useful it can be.

While more complex flowcharts may use up to fifteen different symbols, the simple flowchart of Figure 1 uses only three. These are:

0 The decision box represented by the diamond shape. This box represents a question whose answers are either yes or no. For the flowcharts in this book if the answer is yes leave the box from the left, if the answer is no, leave the box from the right (as indicated by the respective arrows. In other books, and among programmers, when no arrows are shown, the flow is assumed to be from left to right and from top to bottom.

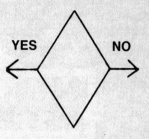

0 The direction box represented by the rectangle. It contains an instruction.

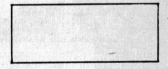

0 A line with an arrow indicates the program flow. By following the arrow and line you can easily see the sequence to follow when going from one box (or instruction and decision) to another. Arrows can point up, down, right, or left.

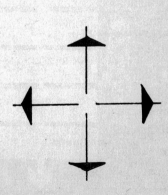

FIGURE 2.1 FLOWCHART OF TELEPHONE CALL

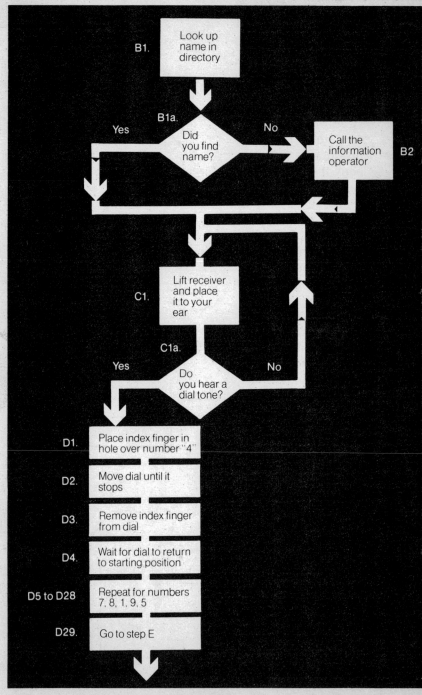

FIGURE 2.1 (Contd.)   **FLOWCHART OF TELEPHONE CALL (Contd.)**

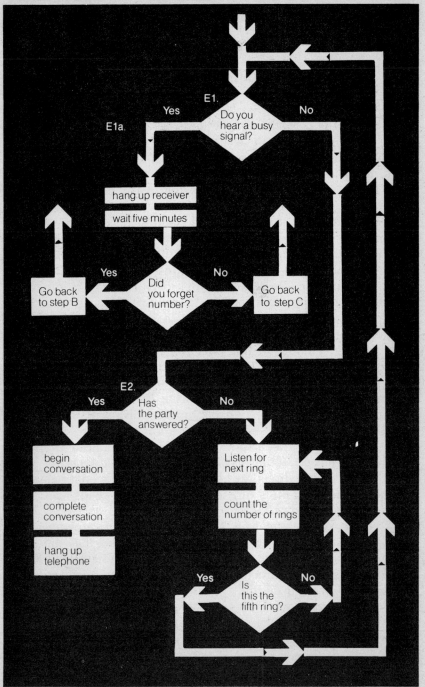

Analyzing the Procedure

Using the flowchart in Figure 2.1 and the set of instructions previously written, let us analyze the program's structure to see what else can be learned about thinking in computer terms.

The program sometimes calls for instructions to be repeated. An example is in part E1a. where the instruction is to go back to step B or C depending on whether or not you forgot the telephone number. In order to keep track of these detours, each instruction must be given a unique label. (To simplify the example, we used alphabetic and numeric labels and in order to avoid cumbersome notation did not label each instruction. Please consider this author's license in the interest of clarity.)

Referring to flowchart instruction B1, we are told to look up the name in the directory. The instruction is contained within a rectangular "direction" box.

What do we do once the name is looked up? The line and arrow combination coming from the bottom of the box points down and connects to the decision diamond B1a. Here a specific yes or no question is asked. If the answer is yes, the arrows direct the program to the direction box C1. If the answer is no, the arrow directs the program to the direction box B2. After the operator is called, the program is directed to box C1. All roads lead to the direction box C1.

Let us pause here to analyze how well the program planned for contingencies. We have assumed that the individual's telephone number is definitely available from either the directory or the telephone operator. However, what if the individual is located in a different city? Unless you have the directory for that city or call the information operator from that city, you will not get the correct telephone number. The box B2 assumes that you received the correct number, if you didn't you can't go to C1 (lift the receiver). For a long distance telephone call the program will be stalled at B2, the system will "hang up" as they say in computer jargon.

While this program may be successfully used hundreds of times for local calls, just imagine what will happen to the poor bloke who inadvertently tries it for a long distance call. Clearly, the program should include a warning to users: THIS PROGRAM WAS DESIGNED FOR LOCAL CALLS ONLY; DO NOT USE THIS PROGRAM FOR LONG DISTANCE CALLS. If the program's designer forsees this problem, he will include the warning, if not, a program that everyone thought was perfect will "suddenly" have developed a "bug" and everyone will shout computer error. Was it an error or an oversight, and whose error was it?

Continuing through the program, look at the relationship between boxes C1 and C1a. The program instructs us to repeat lifting the receiver until we hear a dial tone. Notice how the lines and arrows connecting the right exit from C1a to C1 then back to C1a form an enclosure as you loop around this program path until you do hear a dial tone? In fact such an instruction grouping is called a "program loop."

Just above the C1, C1a loop there's also an enclosure of lines formed by the B1a, B2 combination. This latter combination is not a program loop. All arrows direct the program to C1, the program does not "loop" around repetitively in this case.

Another loop in the program is the E1, E2, back to E1 combination. Note that within this loop there is a smaller loop in E2 (listen for next ring, count number of rings, is this the fifth ring)?

Computer Language

Because you can understand the preceding procedure and flowchart, you may be thinking that it's not a computer program. In the strict sense of the term, it isn't in a language that the computer can understand. However, the procedure and its individual steps are clear. As a result all that's needed at this point is the translation.

Please bear in mind, however, that you did not require any special training or experience to understand the procedure. The truly important part of the programming effort has already been accomplished. From here on, we're really just concerned with finer points. Of course these finer points are extremely important; without them the computer can't do its job. However, we cannot overemphasize the fact that nothing can happen until the human designer specifies each step that must be performed.

When we were in school, we all listened to our teacher's explanation of grammar, punctuation, spelling, and pronunciation. In order to pass the tests we were given, we all memorized the rules and, in class, obeyed the linguistic rules. After all, we were learning for the future and training to become educated members of our society.

When you left the classroom, however, and engaged in normal conversation with your friends, did you follow the pronunciation rules learned in class? On occasion, most of us still violate the grammatical rules we learned, particularly in our daily conversation.

We tend to pay more attention to spelling and punctuation; perhaps because we are committing ourselves to paper, a permanent medium that records our mistakes.

Even with this extra care, we still make errors. In many businesses, typists spend almost half their time correcting typographical errors.

Interestingly, in spite of all the linguistic errors made in our personal and business lives, we still manage to communicate. When a friend tells you "I ain't goin," you understand the statement as fully as if you were told "I am not going." You'll understand the meaning either way. But, you are a human, not a computer.

The computer is a fusspot. It's worse than the strictest teacher you ever had. Whereas your teacher may have grimaced at your violation of the linguistic rules, or kept you after school, the computer does something much worse; it completely ignores you.

Have you ever been ignored by a teacher or friend? It can be one of the most frustrating experiences you have. There you are waving your arms, shouting at the top of your voice, anxious to get the other person's attention so you can "get it off your chest" or "put in your two cents." Exasperation and frustration, agony and high blood pressure, these are images that come to mind when the object of our attention is inattentive.

Because all instructions to a computer ultimately become electrical signals, the computer demands that you strictly obey all linguistic rules. To a computer isn't and ain't is as different as turnips and elephants. A computer designed to turn on a light when it receives signal 1234, may end up shutting off all the faucets in the building if it receives the signal 1235.

Computer languages have rules of grammar as well as rules of punctuation. Usually a computer is designed to handle a number of languages. While we will not discuss any specific computer language here, we do want to emphasize that the rules must be obeyed.

As an aside, various private and government agencies have attempted to define standard languages for all computers. These attempts have been successful to some extent, but it's still a pretty general rule that a computer program written to operate on one brand of computer will not operate on another.

To demonstrate the use of computer languages, we've designed a simple set of instructions that can represent the telephone dialing program. While we'll introduce additional instructions later, for the present, we'll discuss the following instructions.

Instruction	Meaning
PRINT (. . . . .)	Print the statement enclosed in parenthesis. For example, PRINT (hello). The computer will cause the statement "hello" to be printed on its printing device.
DO (. . . . .)	Do the operation indicated within the parenthesis. For example, DO (hang up receiver). The computer will hang up the receiver.
IF (. . . .) THEN (. . .)	If the condition specified in the first parenthesis is true, then do what is instructed in the second set of parenthesis. If the condition is not true, then just go to the next instruction. For example, IF (today is Tuesday) THEN (pay the rent).
MAKE (. . . .) EQUAL TO (. . .)	Set the item named in the first parenthesis equal to the item named in the second set. For example,

DATA (. . . . .)

GO TO (. . . .)

END

MAKE (counter) EQUAL TO (7). The computer will assign the number 7 to the item called "counter."

The numbers within the parenthesis are the data that will be manipulated. For example, DATA (9,25,33). If this were a program dealing with the ages of your relatives, then your brother might be 9 years old, while your uncle and aunt might be 25 and 33, respectively. If you wanted to change the telephone number in the example, you would express the new number as (for example) DATA (4,8,4,7,9,3,2).

Go to the instruction indicated within the parenthesis. For example, GO TO (step C). The computer will implement step C as the next instruction.

The end of the program has been reached. This tells the computer that your program is finished and it can remove your job from its workload.

A computer program consists of a series of statements. Each statement is written on a single line. In addition, each statement must be assigned a unique "line number." In the following, the telephone dialing program is written as a formal computer program using the instructions defined above. We'll discuss the program later, but first go through each step, refer to the flowchart for guidance on the program's flow, and refer to the previous English language programs discussed earlier.

110	PRINT (This program is valid only for local calls; do not use this program for long distance calls)
120	DO (locate name)
130	DO (look up name in directory)
140	IF (name found) THEN (go to 160)
150	DO (call information operator)
160	DO (lift receiver)
170	DO (place receiver to ear)
180	IF (you hear dial tone) THEN (go to 200)
190	GO TO 160
200	MAKE (counter) EQUAL TO (7)
210	DATA (4,7,8,1,2,9,5)
220	MAKE (A) EQUAL TO (next number in DATA sequence)
230	DO (place finger in hole over number "A")
240	DO (move dial until it stops)
250	DO (remove index finger from dial)
260	DO (wait for dial to return to starting position)
270	DO (subtract the number 1 from counter)
280	IF (counter equals zero) THEN (go to 300)

290   GO TO 220

300   IF (you hear a busy signal) THEN (go to 310)

305   GO TO 350

310   DO (hang up receiver)

320   DO (wait five minutes)

330   IF (you forgot number) THEN (go to 130)

340   IF (you remember number) THEN (go to 160)

350   IF (party on other end answers) THEN (go to 400)

360   DO (listen for next ring)

370   DO (add one to number of rings)

380   IF (number of rings equals five) THEN (go to 310)

390   GO TO 360

400   DO (begin conversation)

410   DO (complete conversation)

420   DO (hang up telephone)

430   END

Now, let's analyze the program.

Notice that each instruction is numbered in ascending order. The computer (unless instructed differently) always steps through each instruction in ascending order. For example, the first instruction to be performed is number 110, then 120, 130, and 140.

At instruction 140, if the name is found, the computer is instructed to jump over to instruction 160 and continue with 170 and 180 in sequence; instruction 150 will be bypassed. However, if the name is not found, then the computer performs the next instruction after 140 which is 150 and the sequence continues through 160, 170, 180.

Now instruction 180 is another contingency. If you hear a dial tone then jump to 200, otherwise do the next instruction which is 190. Instruction 190 sends the computer back to instruction 160 from where the program continues in sequence. Until a dial tone is heard the program loops from 190 to 160 and repeats, this is exactly the loop C1 to C1a we discussed when studying the flowchart of Figure 2.1.

When the dial tone is finally heard, program control picks up at instruction 200. The program will step through instructions 200 to 290. Later we'll discuss this portion in more detail since it is the repetitive subroutine for dialing the telephone number. However, at this point we want to restrict the discussion to the procedure for stepping through the program. Note, however, that the group of instructions 200 to 290 is another loop, the program loops through this sequence until "counter equals zero" as specified in instruction 280, at which point instruction 290 is bypassed and control picks up at instruction 300.

Let's return to the program's beginning for a look at some of its highlights.

Perhaps you've already noticed that each instruction number skips ten units. That is, the first instruction is 110 while the second is 120, then 130, etc. We use intervals of ten as a convenience. We could have used intervals of twenty, of two, or simply used random numbers (providing that the numbers are in the same order as the program flow).

The reason for using intervals of ten is it allows the program to be corrected if a mistake was initially made. This is demonstrated in the sequence of instructions 300, 305, 310. When the program was originally written, the statement "GO TO 350" was missing. Rather than renumber each line, the missing line was designated 305 and inserted accordingly. In the overwhelming number of cases, no program is correct the first time it's written. Programmers try the program on the computer, errors usually occur, and modifications are required. By leaving space between line numbers this program, "editing" becomes less burdensome (it's never simple).

The first instruction 110, prints the warning that the program is invalid for long distance calls. Strictly speaking, the program will work without this warning. However, to assure that the program is only used to tackle jobs for which it was intended, such warnings are good practice. Some programs have more elaborate statements describing their operation. Because the descriptions sometimes run to several page documents, statements of this nature are referred to as "documentation."

Adequate documentation of program details as well as the overall process flow is extremely important, particularly in the realm of the personal computer. One of the interesting outcomes of the personal computer revolution is the growth of the personal computer programmer. Individual entrepreneurs ranging from intelligent high school students to professional systems analysts advertise a wide range of software available for use on personal computers. These advertisements appear in a variety of new magazines that keep pace with the latest developments in the field. The software available from this market is usually cheaper than similar packages from a recognized vendor. However, in the long run it can be more expensive, particularly if adequate documentation is not available.

Documentation is extremely important not only as a warning to avoid misuse of the program, but also as a historical record. If the programmer has left the company, or six months have gone by, and a change to the program is required, unless clear documentation is available, serious problems can develop. Programs are not read like short stories. It's not easy for a person unfamiliar with the program to follow its flow unless provided with written statements such as those appearing in instruction 110 and a flowchart.

As a rule of thumb, you should be capable of understanding the program's overall features from the documentation and flowchart even if you're unfamiliar with the specific instruction logic.

Subroutines

Sometimes people refer to computer programs as "routines." As a result, smaller programs imbedded within a larger program go by the name of "subroutine."

Instructions 200 through 290 comprise a subroutine within the telephone dialing program. This subroutine furnishes all the instructions required for actually dialing the seven digit telephone number.

Subroutines are used to simplify writing programs so there's less chance of error. They consist of a set of instructions that are frequently used by the main program. Usually, the instructions are written at the end of the main program. However, when an instruction within the main program calls for the subroutine, computer processing automatically jumps to the first instruction in the subroutine. After the subroutine is completed, control passes back to the next instruction of the main program.

As an example, let's look at a modification of the telephone dialing program. We'll change instruction 180 so that control is passed to instruction 195 (a new instruction that was not in the original program). Instruction 195 calls a subroutine named DIAL. Since the subroutine is written at the end of the program, the next instruction in the main program will be 300. Here's how the affected instructions would look.

    180   IF (you hear dial tone) THEN (go to 195)
    190   GO TO 160

195   CALL (subroutine DIAL)

300   IF (you hear a busy signal) THEN (go to 310)

In the interest of brevity we won't rewrite subroutine DIAL since it is exactly the set of instructions 200 to 290. The instruction calls up a subroutine and causes the computer to automatically jump to the first instruction in the subroutine. Then if all instructions within the subroutine are sequenced properly, the computer steps through and jumps back to the main program.

Another benefit derived from the subroutine concept is more understandable programs. The single instruction 195 replaced ten instructions (200 to 290) thus shortening the program listing. Note that the computer still must perform each instruction, but the human reader will find it simpler to read only one line of coding rather than the original ten.

Still another benefit of the subroutine concept is that another program can refer to an existing subroutine and avoid duplicate program writing. There are many different situations in which a telephone is dialed. As long as the programmer is aware that subroutine DIAL is available, he can simply write an instruction similar to 195 and avoid extra effort and its accompanying potential for error.

As a matter of fact the telephone dialing program consists of a number of subroutines. Here's how it can be written using subroutines.

110   PRINT (This program is valid only for local calls; do not use this program for long distance calls)

120   DO (locate name)

130   DO (look up name in directory)

140   IF (name found) THEN (go to 160)

150   DO (call information operator)

160   DO (lift receiver)

170   DO (place receiver to ear)

180   IF (you hear dial tone) THEN (go to 195)

190   GO TO 160

195   CALL (subroutine DIAL)

300   IF (you hear a busy signal) THEN (go to 307)

305   GO TO 350

307   CALL (subroutine BUSY)

350   IF (party on other end answers) THEN (go to 395)

355   CALL (subroutine RINGING)

395   CALL (subroutine CONVERSATION)

430   END

DIAL

200   MAKE (counter) EQUAL TO (7)

210   DATA (4,7,8,1,2,9,5)

220   MAKE (A) EQUAL TO (next number in sequence)

230   DO (place finger in hole over number "A")

240   DO (move dial until it stops)

250   DO (remove index finger from dial)

260   DO (wait for dial to return to starting position)

270   DO (subtract the number "1" from counter)

280   IF (counter equals zero) THEN (go to 295)

290   GO TO 220

295   GO TO 307

BUSY

310	DO (hang up receiver)
320	DO (wait five minutes)
330	IF (you forgot number) THEN (go to 130)
340	IF (you remember number) THEN (go to 160)
345	GO TO 350

RINGING

360	DO (listen for next ring)
370	DO (add one to number of rings)
380	IF (number of rings equals five) THEN (go to 307)
390	GO TO 360

CONVERSATION

400	DO (begin conversation)
410	DO (complete conversation)
420	DO (hang up telephone)
425	GO TO 430

Central Processor

The central processor is the brains of the outfit. It incorporates the electronic logic components that actually perform the instructions specified by the program. All data eventually flows through the central processing unit. Indeed, this piece of the computer system gets its name from its function.

Central because everything hooks up to this unit either directly or through an intermediary control unit. Just as the record turntable, radio tuner, tape drive, and microphone of a hi-fi system hook up to the amplifier, the computer's memory and input and output devices hook up to the central processor.

Processor because this unit performs all the actions and operations that lead to the specified end. These actions and operations are the process.

The central processor is a hardware unit. It will not function, however, unless it is given a proper set of instructions. As an analogy, let's briefly discuss a concept somewhat popular among investigators of psychic phenomena. The concept distinguishes between the brain and the mind.

The brain is a physical organ of the body. It contains cells, tissue and a variety of other biological structures. We can say that the brain falls into the hardware category.

The mind is a composite of thoughts and ideas. It's a concept without physical manifestation. You can't see or touch a mind. Many investigators have explored the unconscious, but nobody has ever seen it. The computer is a fairly mundane subject compared to the mind. Nevertheless, it's useful to make the analogy and point out that, in many ways, the mind is to the brain as the software program is to the hardware central processor.

So then, just as the human needs an active brain and an intelligent working mind to function, the central processor requires a proper set of program instructions.

Many Options, Many Choices

Central processors come with a variety of capabilities. The smart shopper will select a system that has the features required to perform the immediate job at hand and additional growth potential for future applications. Since you are spending money for every feature, only select the features you need.

Frequently, people ask the experts to name the best computer available. Unfortunately, there is no such thing as the best computer; it really depends on the application you have in mind.

If someone asked you to name the best automobile or truck available, what would you answer? Perhaps the individual intends to use the automobile for racing. In that case a four-door sedan that comfortably fits a family of five would not satisfy his requirements. On the other hand, the souped-up sports car would be a total failure if used by farmers to transport their produce from the farm to the marketplace.

The sports car, the sedan, the truck, each has an engine, wheels, and basically the same components. However, they are quite different in size and scope, depending on the application. The same holds for computers, and, in particular, central processors.

Earlier, we mentioned the analogy between the computer's central processor and the hi-fi system's amplifier. Let's explore this analogy further.

The amplifier does not control the hi-fi system in the same way as the central processor controls the computer system. However, the amplifier is a central piece of equipment. All electrical signals pass through the amplifier. The amplifier strengthens the signals so that they are sufficiently powerful to move the loudspeaker components and thus produce sound.

Usually, the amplifier is housed in a chassis that has a variety of additional features. We want to focus our analogy in this area of the amplifier chassis.

Depending on the sophistication of the hi-fi system, there can be a few dials and lights on the amplifier chassis, or for the hi-fi buff, there can be many. Here's a possible potpourri.

0   Selection switch for turntable, tape, or cassette. Depending on the recording device you're playing from, you will turn the appropriate switch. Of course, some systems do not offer all three options. Some systems are simply phonographs, or cassette players, etc. In these cases a selection switch is not provided since the system dictates a single choice.

0   am/fm radio selection switch. Additionally, we can imagine that some enterprising manufacturer has already produced, or is close to producing, shortwave radio and citizen band options.

0   Automatic volume control so that the volume

maintains a constant unchanging level. Some people claim they can detect very minor volume fluctuations and, as a result, are perfectly willing to pay the additional cost in order to avoid this problem.

0   Automatic frequency control for the radio components. This feature is the one we find most exotic. Many systems have hypnotic green lights and other displays that indicate when the dial setting is exactly on the proper frequency. In addition, the control makes automatic adjustments to return the frequency to its proper value whenever it strays.

0   Recording or playback switch. Many hi-fi systems allow you to play the phonograph and at the same time to record on a tape or cassette.

0   Strobe light feature. This is a relatively new invention in the history of high fidelity. It plugs into the system in the same way as a loudspeaker. However, instead of producing sound, it produces lights of varying colors. The lights blink in rhythm with the music and the colors change in rhythm with the volume. When you think about it, this optical light show is a somewhat peculiar option to provide for a system originally engineered to reproduce sound. However, it simply proves the point that, at times, people can request the strangest options. This applies for hi-fi equipment, automobiles, and also computers.

What Does the Central Processor Do?

The central processor does what it's told to do. Do not forget that the central processor "brain" is simply a pile of wires and electrical circuits. Without the program "mind" the central processor does nothing.

One question that's usually raised at this point is how does the central processor do what it's supposed to do? How can instructions written on paper control electrical signals in a piece of hardware composed of electrical logic circuits? Many procedures are available for transforming the instructions into electrical signals. While we do not want to get bogged down in these details, it would be worth a slight digression to explain how the "mind" and "brain" join together.

A simple procedure for entering the program's instructions into the central processor is to use a typewriter keyboard. You're probably familiar with electric typewriters. When you hit the keyboard, you are producing a coded electrical signal that causes one of the alphabetic or numeric characters to strike the paper.

In a similar fashion, as each instruction is typed, electrical signals are produced. These signals are captured by an appropriate memory device. While we'll discuss the details of various memory devices in later chapters, you can think of them as many batteries. You're certainly familiar with the fact that batteries store electrical energy. For computers, it was found that magnetic storage is more suitable. Here, the electrical signals magnetize small pieces of iron (each shaped like a doughnut). The little magnets become magnetized under the direction of the incoming electrical signals as determined by the original program.

The central processor must analyze the little memory magnets and interpret their information. To the credit of modern day computer designers who are themselves the technological descendants of previous electrical engineers, the electrical and magnetic signaling and interpretation actually works.

The central processor can understand each instruction and after interpreting the instruction execute its command. Now let us discuss the central processor's role in a little more detail.

The central processor is like a band leader. Whereas the band leader must conduct the operation of perhaps a ten-piece band, the central processor conducts the operation of a variety of input and output devices, the arithmetic logic units, and the flow of data and instructions from memory to the appropriate logic units. Just as the band leader operates under the direction of the musical score, the central processor operates under the direction of the program.

The central processor "reads" the information from the storage units. The information consists of instructions as well as data. For example, if the instructions are to add three numbers, the actual numbers involved constitute the data.

After the central processor "reads" the information, it transfers or "moves" the instructions and data to special hardware sections called "logic units" where the data is manipulated. After an arithmetic operation is performed, the data can be returned to storage or to one of the output devices.

The central processing unit does more than simple arithmetic. Besides addition, subtraction, multiplication, and division, the central processor performs comparisons, makes decisions, and handles some general housekeeping chores.

For example, before instructions or data can be entered from a keyboard, the central processor must be ready for its acceptance. The central processor will signal the terminal when it is ready. In addition, when the central processor is moving data between input and output devices, the memory, and the logic units, it must maintain a constant vigilance to make sure that the correct piece of data or instruction is removed from the correct memory location and transferred back to memory or correctly outputted on a printer or display. While it may

appear that the central processor is in danger of being
overwhelmed by this flurry of activity, as we'll see, it
really has everything under control.

Functional Components

From the functional point of view, the central processor requires a control unit, an arithmetic logic unit,
and a variety of storage registers. Specific construction
details will vary among different manufacturers. For
example, in some cases some storage registers will reside
in the control unit while others will be in a separate
portion of the central processor.

The control unit is the computer's traffic policeman. It
controls the flow of information, ensuring that the correct
data is transferred among the proper computer components. In addition, the control unit keeps track of transfer
speeds, making sure that data travels within the processor at the proper transfer rates.

The situation is comparable to the traffic policeman at
a large intersection. He must stop northbound traffic in
order to enable eastbound traffic to proceed. While
northbound traffic is stopped, other automobiles are
moving along to the end of the line. The northbound
traffic line will grow in size. If it backs up too far it will
interfere with traffic at another intersection. As a result,
the traffic policeman must keep track of the length of time
the northbound traffic is halted so that it can be restarted
before a major traffic jam develops at another intersection.

While the control unit is dealing with instructions and
data, rather than with automobiles, it is performing an
analogous function. The control unit arranges for information to be sent to the proper output device if it's to be

displayed, or to the arithmetic logic unit if it's to be manipulated.

The arithmetic logic unit performs arithmetic. It is comparable to a calculator. Indeed just as calculators range from the very simple to the more elaborate, depending on the computer system, the arithmetic logic unit will offer more or less capability.

All arithmetic logic units furnish the addition capability. Recall, that as a child, before you learned to multiply five times four, you solved the problem by adding five to itself four times. Multiplication is simply another form of addition. In fact, division and subtraction are also based on addition. As a result, if you have a device that can add, you can also perform multiplication, division, and subtraction. Of course these other operations will be performed more quickly if subtractors, multipliers, and dividers are included in the logic unit in addition to the adder. On the other hand, these special features do increase the cost. As a result, when making a judgement on the necessity for these extra units, you should ask yourself whether the additional cost is warranted. There is no definitive answer to this tradeoff, it truly depends on your particular circumstance. What is considered a luxury for one situation can be an absolute necessity for another.

Storage registers are special memory units that help inform the control unit what to do and where to transfer information. Whereas regular computer memories store large amounts of information, storage registers are limited to specific items. For an analogy, if the regular storage is the book, then the one line table of contents entries can represent the storage registers.

Just as some books have separate tables of contents for illustrations and tables, computers offer a variety of storage registers. The number of registers can range from one or two on through more than one hundred. We'll discuss a few of the more elementary types.

FIGURE 3.1   STORAGE REGISTER OPERATION

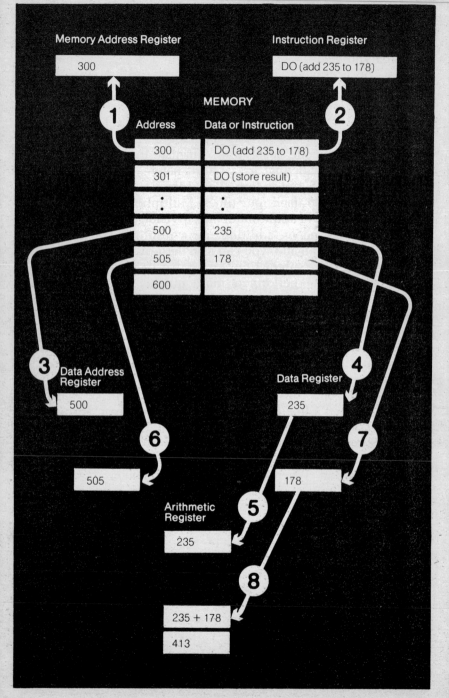

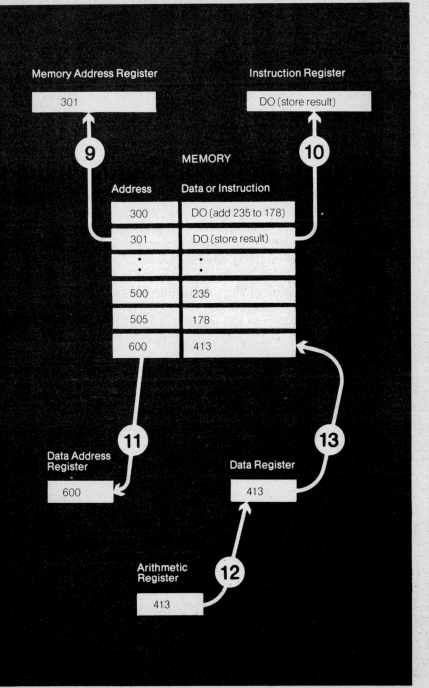

Recall that during the discussion of the telephone dialing program we pointed out that each instruction is labelled with a unique numerical designation. We also discussed the sequence of the program flow, that unless the program specifies a GO TO or IF, THEN instruction, program control always goes to the next instruction in sequence.

The central processor keeps track of the instruction numbers by means of a "memory address register." This register holds the number of the instruction being executed. If the instruction is branch (GO TO, etc.) then the next number to appear in the memory address register will be the instruction number of the branch to instruction. If there is no branch, then the next instruction in the program list will be designated.

As an illustration of the memory address register's operation, let's look at the execution of a portion of the telephone dialing program.

130   DO (look up name in directory)

140   IF (name found) THEN (go to 160)

150   DO (call information operator)

160   DO (lift receiver)

170   DO (place receiver to ear)

During program execution, the memory address register will store the following instruction addresses:

130

140

If the name is found the following sequence:

160

170

If the name is not found the following sequence:

150

160

170

Whereas the memory address register tells the system *where* the current instruction is to be found, it does not tell the system *what* the instruction is. For the *what* is part of the operation, the central processor contains the "instruction register."

The instruction register stores the instruction currently being executed. While at first sight, this may not appear terribly significant, we must pause to emphasize a very important point. Namely, there is only one instruction register. As a result, the computer executes only one instruction at a time. While it may appear to the outside world that the computer is performing many instructions simultaneously, this is not the case. The central processor logic and control units are totally devoted to performing the single instruction currently residing in the instruction register. However, because the processor executes the instruction within one millionth of a second, and up to one million instructions can be executed within one second, it appears that everything is happening at once.

Up to this point we have not discussed the computer's main storage components. In fact we're reserving a complete discussion for a later chapter. However, for now, suffice it to say that the data to be manipulated is stored in a suitable location. By data we mean the various numbers such as payroll dollars, number of employees, number of machine parts, etc. After all, the major use for most computers is to finally perform calculations on business data.

Think of main storage as the "pigeon hole" postal boxes rented by the post office. Each box has a unique number and each box contains an item such as a letter or parcel. In the computer situation, the box is a memory location and the letter is a specific piece of information represented by a number.

When the computer is instructed to for example, add two numbers, it must be told where the numbers are located. In computer terminology, the processor must be told the address of the data to be manipulated.

The "data address register" holds the address of the memory cell that contains the piece of data that will be involved in the arithmetic operation (such as addition or subtraction). The "data register" on the other hand holds the actual number. Both of these registers (data address and data) perform the same function for the data that the memory address and instruction registers perform for the instructions.

Another slight digression here. Earlier, we did not discuss the concept of addresses for data nor where these addresses reside in the program. Remember, our intention is to avoid burdensome programming details while concentrating on the kind of thinking required for programming. Consequently, we will not go into the details, but do want to note that the programmer takes care of specifying addresses for data as well as various other housekeeping details.

To see how these registers control the computer's operation, let's consider steps involved in adding two numbers and storing the result.

Assume that the programmer's housekeeping specified that the number 235 is in memory location 500, the number 178 is in memory location 505, and the sum of these numbers is to be stored in memory location 600. From our point of view, we'll express the program by the following two instructions.

    300   DO (add 235 to 178)

    301   DO (store result)

The sequence of events is illustrated in Figures 3.1 and 3.2 (note that each step is identified by a circled number) and discussed as follows:

- 0 Memory address register will contain 300, the instruction address (step 1)
- 0 Instruction register will contain DO (add), the instruction under execution (step 2)
- 0 Data address register will contain 500, the memory location of the first number (step 3)
- 0 Data register will contain 235, the actual number involved in the addition (step 4)
- 0 The processors electrical circuits now send the contents of the data register to the "arithmetic register," where the actual addition will take place (not at this point, however, since the second number has not yet arrived) (step 5)
- 0 After the first number is sent to the arithmetic register, the processor automatically loads the data address register with the address of the second number (step 6) and the data register with the actual number (step 7)
- 0 Now the processor sends the second number to the arithmetic register (step 8). As the second number arrives, the arithmetic logic unit arranges for the value of the incoming number to be added to the number already residing in the arithmetic register. The contents of the arithmetic register is now the sum of the two numbers: 235 plus 178 equals 413.
- 0 At this point, the addition instruction has been completed, so the memory address register is loaded with the address of the next instruction. Figure 2 picks up the sequence; note that instruction 301 is indicated in the memory address register (step 9).
- 0 The storage instruction is loaded into the instruction register (step 10)

0   Since the final sum is destined for storage loca-
    tion 600, this number is loaded into the data
    address register (step 11)
0   The contents of the arithmetic register is loaded
    into the data register which in turn transfers the
    datum to memory address 600 (steps 12 and 13).

In describing the process for implementing the addition instruction, we introduced the "arithmetic register."
The arithmetic register is the location where each arithmetic operation is actually performed.

Computers vary in the number and type of arithmetic
registers. All computers offer at minimum an addition
register. As we mentioned earlier, every other arithmetic
operation can be performed from a series of additions.
For example, if in the problem just analyzed, we added
the same number to itself the operation would be multiplication by two. If we repeated the addition fifteen
times, then we multiplied the number by fifteen.

In the early days, computers contained only the addition register. Along the way, this register became known
as the "accumulator register"; perhaps because it accumulated the result of successive additions.

In today's computer world, you can obtain separate
arithmetic registers for subtraction, multiplication, and
division. In fact, frequently, these registers are offered as
options so the potential buyer can select only those
registers needed for his particular application.

As with all purchases, the answer to whether or not
you will benefit from these options depends upon the
added cost versus the savings to your operation. Since
these optional registers speed up the arithmetic, they will
enable the computer to handle more arithmetic operations in any given time period. However, if you are not
using your computer system to its full capacity, you may
be able to afford the extra time and the extra registers will
be unnecessary. One good approach is to select a system
that allows the optional registers to be installed at a

future date if your workload develops to a level that requires the additional speed.

Performance is a term used to give an indication of how well a computer does its job. Unfortunately it is not really a well-defined term. Performance depends to a large measure on the specific application. However, computer people have learned to recognize the major factors that contribute to a computer's performance. While a specific formula is not available, we can discuss some of these ingredients and see how they affect performance.

At the risk of redundancy, we remind you that the computer operates sequentially. Only one step is carried out at a time. Indeed the previously discussed addition instruction was implemented by eight separate transfers of information between memory and registers (see Figure 3.1 for a reminder). Each of these steps is called a "cycle." Depending on how the computer was designed, each instruction is usually performed in more than one cycle (generally, less than ten).

When referring to the central processor's speed, computer people speak of the "cycle time," the time required for the central processor to complete one cycle. We may say that our addition instruction required eight cycle times to run to completion. In a different system, the same instruction may require only three or four cycles (perhaps the computer designer was more efficient) or it may require nine or ten cycles. The point we want to stress is that speed depends upon how the instruction is performed (number of cycles) and how fast the computer operates (cycle time).

Central processor cycle times range from less than one half to several microseconds. A microsecond is one millionth of a second. Stated another way, a central processor with a one microsecond cycle time will perform one million cycles in one second. If this central processor requires ten cycles to perform a particular instruction, it can perform the instruction one hundred thousand times each second. On the other hand another central processor with a cycle time of two microseconds, but capable of carrying out the instruction in five cycles will also perform one hundred thousand instructions each second. In this specific instance, while each central processor has a different cycle time, they both implement the addition instruction in the same time.

To give you a somewhat fuller understanding of this relation between speed, cycle time, and number of cycles the following lists some representative examples.

Processor	Cycle time	Number of cycles required to complete instruction	Actual time to complete instruction
A	1.5 microseconds	4	6 microseconds
B	1.5 microseconds	6	9 microseconds
C	2 microseconds	2	4 microseconds
D	2 microseconds	3	6 microseconds

Processor A has a faster cycle time than processor C, but since processor C implements the instruction in fewer cycles, it performs the instruction in a shorter time.

We've been discussing processor speeds and have stated that computers can perform hundreds of thousands of instruction executions in just one second. Clearly then, computers are extremely high speed calculating devices. However, there's a catch to all this speed.

When we said the computer can perform hundreds of thousands of instruction executions in one second, we did not mean that in one second the computer can perform one hundred thousand *different* instructions. The computer can perform some combination of one to two hundred instructions repetitively. But the computer does not offer the programmer a menu of one hundred thousand separate instructions to choose from. Such an instruction set would be enormous. You have spoken English all your life and you don't have a vocabulary that comes close to one hundred thousand words. This book which you are now reading does not employ a vocabulary of one hundred thousand words. Indeed, the book does not even come close to having one hundred thousand words.

Computers differ in the number of different instructions offered. Some models provide perhaps fifty separate instructions, others as much as two hundred. The "instruction set" is commonly called an "instruction repertoire." The specific instructions offered depend on the computer's potential application. For example, some systems will offer a multiplication instruction. Other systems, in order to reduce manufacturing costs will offer only the addition instruction; they assume the user will write a program for multiplication based on successive additions.

Whatever the number of instructions in the repertoire, the computer program will consist of some combinations of a fairly limited set. The computer's central processor can process the program over and over again at the rate of about one hundred thousand instruction executions per second, but the process is essentially repeating the same basic information.

We want to emphasize at this point that the computer works best when it's assigned repetitive tasks. It's practically impossible to program a computer otherwise. After all, a human being is writing the program. In less than a day the computer has gone through as many cycles as the average human being goes through in a complete lifetime.

What is a human equivalent to the computer cycle? While biologists might frown on the following definition, we feel it's safe to say that the heartbeat makes a good human internal clock. After all, before clocks were invented, people did use their pulse beat to keep track of short time intervals. We humans can react within a tenth of a second to some situations, but a second is about the shortest time frame that we can ·comfortably operate within. But to give us humans the benefit of the doubt, let's say that our cycle time is one tenth of a second.

Now the question we'll ask is how many cycles does the average human expend in one lifetime of seventy years? We'll find the answer with some very simple arithmetic.

Each minute contains 60 seconds. An hour contains 60 minutes or 3600 seconds. Since each day contains 24 hours we multiply 3600 seconds per hour by 24 hours per day to find there are 86,400 seconds in each day. Each year contains 365 days (we will not count leap years); so multiply 86,400 seconds per day by 365 days per year to get 31,540,000 seconds per year (that's about thirty-one million seconds per year).

How many seconds in seventy years? Multiply about 31 million by 70 to get about two and one quarter billion (2.208 billion to be more mathematically specific). Now since each human cycle is one tenth of a second, we multiply the previous number by ten to get a grand total of 22 billion cycles for a human lifetime of seventy years.

Twenty-two billion of anything seems like a pretty big number. But let's explore this further. If it takes a human being seventy years to go through twenty-two billion cycles, how long does it take a computer?

We've already pointed out that a computer can go through one million cycles in one second. The computer will go through twenty-two billion cycles in twenty-two thousand seconds. Remember that a single day has about eighty-six thousand seconds, so twenty-two thousand seconds is about one quarter of a day, or to be more specific, 6.14 hours.

Let's say that a cycle represents one thought. If you translated every thought you have in your lifetime into a computer program, the computer can process the program in just six hours. All your hopes, dreams, struggles, joys; condense to six hours.

On the other hand, various human beings called programmers spend complete forty-hour weeks writing programs for computers. Moreover, most computers operate at least eight hours a day and put in a five-day work week. What kind of processing are these computers performing? Why doesn't a computer run out of work after a week's operation (the equivalent of six human lifetimes)?

The computer does not run out of work because it performs the same task over and over again. Recall the telephone dialing program discussed earlier. It took a human being roughly one million times longer to write the program than it took the computer to execute the program by dialing one telephone number. However, it doesn't make sense to spend time writing a program that will be executed only once. One can create a list of many telephone numbers (say all the telephones in New York City) and instruct the computer to repeat the telephone dialing program for each number. In this case the computer will be performing the same program perhaps one million times,' but the programmer will be required to write only one program.

Repetition is the key to efficient computer utilization. One programmer writes one program for calculating payroll. The computer repeatedly performs the same calculation for one hundred or one thousand employees fifty-two times (for the fifty-two weeks in each year).

Processor Construction

Let's discuss your hi-fi set for a while. It's probably made from transistors. On the other hand, your television set is most likely constructed from electronic tubes. What's the difference between transistors and tubes, and does it really matter anyway?

Your hi-fi set will produce good music whether or not it's constructed from transistors. The same is true for your television. From the functional point of view, the difference between tubes or transistors is not terribly significant. However, your transistor radio is much more portable and costs considerably less than a comparable radio made from vacuum tubes. (Many of you readers may be too young to remember that there was a time, not very long ago, when the ball point pen and television did not exist and radios were large bulky boxes made from vacuum tubes.)

While the final sound produced by a tube constructed radio or hi-fi set may sound just as good as one constructed from transistors, there are many other conveniences offered by the transistor construction. Reliability is an important consideration. Vacuum tubes burn out; just think of the last time you called in the television repairman. It's almost inevitable that one of the problems was a tube that needed replacing. This is a fairly infrequent occurrence with transistorized radios.

Transistors also operate more quickly. When you turn on a radio or other device constructed from vacuum tubes, there's usually a minute delay before things start working (the vacuum tubes are getting hot). Because of their construction and other properties, transistors do not require this "warmup" period. As a result, when you turn on a transistor you immediately hear sound.

Transistors cost less to produce than do vacuum tubes. In addition, it's easier and as a result, less costly to fabricate a device from transistors than from vacuum tubes. So while the music may be the same, different types of construction do have an impact on cost, portability, speed, convenience, and flexibility. Indeed through these factors, the *how* of computer construction has played a major role in the computer's history and construction.

Over the years, professionals in the industry have referred to "computer generations."

The first generation began in the early 1950s with the introduction by Univac and IBM of computers for commercial business applications. This generation of computers was constructed from vacuum tubes. As a result, their processing tended to be considerably slower than the microsecond cycle times offered by current systems. In addition, because these computers required a considerable number of tubes for their construction, they were physically large machines that required high power consumption. Frequently, vacuum tubes would malfunction and, as a result, considerable time was spent in getting the computer to operate at the expense of time spent in actually processing data.

Because the field of computers was new, trained personnel were not available. In these exciting times, the professionals were inventing procedures and methods for running a computer installation and at the same time gaining experience in implementing them. Highly skilled personnel were required for writing programs, operating the computer, and providing maintenance when they malfunctioned.

If you contemplated using a computer during that first generation, you could expect to spend considerable dollars. The final bill for personnel and equipment could run in the millions of dollars. It's not surprising then, that only mammoth commercial businesses or government agencies had the resources to support a first generation computer installation.

In 1959, IBM launched the second generation of the computer industry with a system constructed from transistors. It was more compact than its predecessors, offered faster processing, and more reliability. As more individuals gained experience in computer programming and operations, the cost of running a computer installation decreased and the use of computers became more widespread. In the second generation, a firm did not have to be that important to justify the need for a computer; however, the firm still had to be large.

System growth was another problem that people began to recognize. As a firm added more and more jobs to its computer, the system would become overloaded. At that time, manufacturers did not offer very much upward growth. Instead of obtaining additional memory, or a faster processor, the user was faced with getting an entirely new and larger computer system. Typically this meant retraining all personnel and writing completely new programs since the new computer would most likely have a completely different instruction set from that of the old computer.

In 1965, IBM introduced its System 360 family of computers. System 360 represented an important advance into the third generation. The system's introduction provided a catalyst for the computer industry to establish a consistent set of design and operating goals that continues to play a major role in the philosophy of computer usage today.

The other major computer manufacturers also introduced comparable systems in the late 1960s. The third generation systems offered further advances in construction technology. However, perhaps more significantly, this generation of computers offered the commercial user considerably more flexibility at lower cost than did the second generation computers. The computer was now brought within reach of the medium-sized business. It began to take its place in business as just another tool used in day-to-day activity.

From the hardware point of view, third generation computers offered "miniaturization" and "integrated circuitry." In the second generation computer, individual transistors were soldered to connecting wires. The transistors were little cylindrical cans with about one-quarter inch sides. By the time the third generation came, technologists developed methods for mounting tiny transistor chips on specially prepared printed circuit boards. Now several logic components could be fabricated on a circuit board of perhaps two inches on a side. Another fabrication method that was in its formative stages, but utilized nevertheless, was "monolithic circuits"—where the circuits were formed from controlled crystal growth; similar to leaving a mug of coffee on the table for several days; eventually, the water will evaporate, leaving a precipitate of dried coffee, milk, and sugar.

The result of these changes was that physically, circuits became even smaller causing fewer soldered connections to break and cause problems. Systems became more reliable, processing speed increased, and manufacturing costs were reduced. So once again the user was offered increased performance at reduced cost. Just like beautiful women, computers were not getting older, they were getting better.

The concept of "compatibility" became important during the third generation. Manufacturers offered families of computers. The intent was that as more work was added to a system and the saturation point reached, the user could exchange the current system for a more powerful member of the computer family. In actual practice the upgrade never worked out quite as smoothly as the manufacturers claimed and the users hoped. However, the process did work more or less to some people's satisfaction, if one considers the problems of earlier generations.

Compatibility considerations among personal computer

components have many similarities to hi-fi stereo systems. While speakers, turntables, and other components can be purchased separately, their electrical features must be matched and the various physical plugs and receptacles must fit. Most personal computers utilize an ordinary television screen for display. Consequently, practically all television video portions are compatible with any personal computer processor/keyboard. Depending on the manufacturer and specific features, magnetic tape cassettes, diskettes, and other peripheral equipment may or may not be compatible. A diskette can be physically compatible because it can plug into a particular processor. However, signal voltages may not be compatible. For example, if the voltages are too high, electrical components can blow out and/or burn up, while insufficient signal power may lead to inoperation of mechanical parts.

Besides the two types of compatibility discussed above (physical plug configuration and signal voltage level), the purchaser of personal computer components should also consider logical compatibility (all components understanding the same signal codes).

As an example, consider a processor/keyboard from one vendor that is intended to function with a magnetic tape cassette from another vendor. Assume that the plugs fit (i.e., processor/keyboard can connect to cassette) and the signal levels are matched. A user at the keyboard can enter an instruction to the processor which in turn will signal the cassette that it is ready to send information. Recall that communication is by means of signal codes of different combinations of on/off, one/zero, etc. As a result, if the processor's signal for "get ready to receive" is on/on/off, then clearly a miscommunication will occur if the cassette's logic language for the same instruction is on/off/on. The final action produced by the cassette will be determined by its understanding of on/on/off. It could simply turn off power, or it could send to rather than receive information from the processor, or it could perform any number of erroneous activities.

Upgrading within a family of computers means that programs written for the previous system would run on the new system with little or no changes (usually this works best when going from a less to a more powerful system). Computers within the same family understand the same language, so the programming staff is not required to spend unproductive time being retrained. All the personnel involved in the computer's operation are usually already familiar with other members in the computer family and, as a result, the transition to a more powerful computer system is smooth.

As a body of computer knowledge and expertise developed, manufacturers began to hire large staffs of maintenance and consulting personnel to help customers in getting started with computers and their ongoing programming and maintenance.

The policy of the computer business used to be to lease rather than to sell equipment. Along with the equipment, the manufacturer provided programming support in the form of consultation and so-called "canned" software packages for performing functions such as payroll, accounts payable, etc. The lease of a computer or family of computers also generally included free maintenance and service by the manufacturer's personnel.

Rather, the cost of the programming and maintenance was not free, but was included in the equipment price. Since the equipment was high priced, these other costs were not significantly high, and as a result, everyone was satisfied. Computer people use the term "bundled" to describe this circumstance where all the factors that contributed to the total cost were added into the equipment price tag.

As the third generation of computers matured, a variety of smaller so-called "third party independents" were formed to sell software, equipment, and maintenance directly to users. (Sometimes the software was called "proprietary.") These independents did not attempt to replace the computer manufacturer's total system with their own. Rather, each "independent" offered a specific product such as an alternative to the manufacturer's magnetic tape drive or an improved accounts receivable program. This system of buying computers is analogous to the buying of automobiles by individuals from the large Detroit manufacturers. Here, there exists the option to purchase radio and tires from separate dealers rather than from the manufacturers of the cars.

Initially, third party independents found difficulty in gaining user acceptance. "Bundling" was a major road-block. The user was already leasing a complete package with a single bundled price tag. Since all the extras were "free" he could not cancel any part of the system to realize a cost savings when using a third party replace-ment. The independents organized and brought the ques-tion before the courts. They contended that "bundling" was a monopolistic practice that resulted in restraint of trade. The courts agreed to some extent, and as a result, "unbundling" was introduced.

The majority of users still elect to lease bundled systems. However, "unbundling" created a sufficiently large potential customer base to lead to the growth of a vital third party industry. The increased competition provided many opportunities for individuals with good ideas, but limited financial resources to establish busi-ness ventures for implementing their ideas.

The personal computer explosion has brought with it a corresponding availability of "unbundled" software from a host of independent full- and part-time programmers. One reason for the low price of the personal computer is that the manufacturer is relieved of the software development ex-pense. Independent programmers generally write software for systems that have the largest user base. This allows the cost of development to be spread over many units thus lowering the price to the individual user. Sometimes a new and technically better personal computer will appear on the market, but the lack of a sufficient user base may discourage independent programmer activity. Contributing to a new form of vicious circle, a limited program library will inhibit user acceptance, thus keeping a lid on independent program offerings. As a result, while many personal computers are announced, only a few manage to cross the threshold of user/software volume into the realm of a fully supported computer system.

The symbiotic relationship between the computer manufacturer, user, and third party independent produced a chain reaction that led to today's thriving computer industry.

The fourth generation of computers is not as clearly defined as its predecessors. The concept of "generations" was a catchy advertising term introduced at the beginning of the third generation. In order to show users how far the industry had advanced, manufacturers defined the first and second generation computers. This first, second, etc., syndrome is something that we frequently encounter. The doughboys fighting in the Ardennes thought they were participating in the Great War. It was only three decades later when someone coined the term "World War II" that everyone realized the previous war was World War I.

The concept of computer generations, however, was useful. It enabled people to classify and identify problems and find solutions. While the first three generations involved growth from infancy through adolescence to maturity, the fourth generation offered more maturity. As a result, when it began, indeed, whether it has in fact begun, is a question that does not have a clear answer. Perhaps it's best to lay the generation terminology to rest and concentrate on the contemporary generation.

Distributed Minicomputing

During the latter part of the 1950s and early 1960s automobile manufacturers introduced bigger and bigger cars with a variety of features such as automatic transmission, power steering, air conditioning, wrap around windshields, eight-track tape players, flashy chrome, and larger size. With these features also came increased prices and increased fuel consumption.

Some people considered these features to be necessary, others considered them to be frills. The more economical drivers were willing to forego some of the special features for automobiles that cost less. During that time, various European manufacturers introduced compact cars that did not have automatic transmission or power steering. The compact cars were smaller and generally required their operators to be more experienced drivers. However, these cars cost less and gave their owners a feeling that they were getting back to basics.

In the late 1960s a similar trend developed within the computer industry, particularly among scientific programmers. Since they already had a high level of technical expertise and experience, they did not require quite the same support from the manufacturer as did the commercial users. Scientific programming involves a considerable amount of numerical manipulation. Generally, these programs require less elaborate input and output devices and smaller memories.

For scientific programs, one benefits from an essentially stripped down version of the commercial systems. Several manufacturers recognized that they could offer less expensive equipment since their overhead for maintenance and development staff would be reduced. These systems were the analogue of the compact car. They required a sophisticated user who was willing to accept lower priced hardware and forego extensive manufacturer support.

At the same time that scientific computers were finding customers, the women's fashion industry was introducing the miniskirt. Even the most studious computer technologist will take notice of a well turned ankle and the shapely thigh barely covered by the miniskirt's hem. In a marriage of industry advertising ploys, someone in the computer industry coined the term "minicomputer" to describe the small scale scientific computers. The computer industry is more faithful to its children than is the fashion industry. Whereas the miniskirt passed into memory (no doubt fondly) the minicomputer is still with us.

The ladies' hemlines were lowered in a succession of forgettable fashions whose two most renowned members were the midiskirt and maxiskirt. This provided an opportunity for minicomputer manufacturers to advertise that some of their systems were larger than minicomputers but smaller than large systems. The large minicomputer was called the midicomputer, and the next largest was called the maxicomputer.

Occasionally, some people still refer to the midicomputer and maxicomputer, but these designations have fallen into disuse. The minicomputer, however, is still in use today. Indeed, with advances in technology and methodology, many minicomputers that are in today's marketplace are more powerful than earlier large scale systems and they are considerably lower priced.

One major contribution of the minicomputer is the "dedicated application." In order to justify costwise a large scale computer system, many commercial enterprises developed internal data processing departments to handle a wide variety of applications. These could range from inventory control to payroll to management reports. Because of the cost involved in having these computer systems, there was a considerable drive to keep them busy as much of the time as possible. Obtaining a computer simply to turn on the lights or keep track of petty cash would have been the height of folly considering the cost involved.

Since the minicomputer was a low cost computer with less varied capabilities, it could be sensibly used for a single application. Instead of all the branches of a large firm sending their data processing jobs to a centrally located large computer at the main office, the firm could now "distribute" minicomputers among its branches. These minicomputers used for business applications are often called "small business computers." They are not computers for small business, but are small computers for business applications.

Through the years, circuit building technology has improved to the point where many electronic components are truly microscopic in nature. Computers built from the microcircuits are called "microcomputers" or "microprocessors."

Most systems sold as "home," "personal," or "hobby" computers are built around microprocessors. In many cases the terms "mini" and "micro" are used interchangeably. While we could describe specific differences, it is not terribly important since both terms are more significant from the marketing point of view than from that of the user.

The salesperson in Ruth Janet's Platter Palace will emphasize "micro" if that is what the customer asks for or "mini" if that seems to be the more saleable term. The important point is how well the *total* system (hardware *and* software) will perform the function you need at the proper price.

The low fabrication costs of microcomputer logic components have enabled them to be used as components in a continually growing number of electronic devices and systems. Along with the ability to distribute the logic, this latest revolution has enabled more businesses to distribute their data processing among their various branches and departments.

The "distributed processing" approach has brought the computer into the office. In this environment, the computer is just another office machine, while in the home the computer is just another appliance. These small computer systems use the "distributed" capabilities of larger capacity and more powerful systems because they are not isolated from each other. Instead, they can be connected to each other through a communications network.

The connecting "communications network" is the familiar telephone line. You can reach almost any point in the world by dialing the right set of numbers on your telephone to carry on a verbal conversation. Rather than send your voice conversation over the telephone lines, you can also send your computer's data the same way. The recipient of this information will be another computer. With this approach various companies are combining distributed computers into networks of various sized computers. The total network is itself one large "computer utility" offering users whatever level of computer compatibility they require at any given time.

A chain of discount stores represents a good example of how distributed processing works. The chain's national headquarters could be located in Chicago. Perhaps it could have three major regions; Eastern headquarters located in New York, Western headquarters located in San Francisco, and Southern headquarters located in Atlanta. Each region may have one hundred stores. National headquarters may want a daily report of the amount of sales from each store. In addition, they may want to know the number of each item sold remaining in inventory. A well run operation requires that each store not have too many or too few of any item. Let's say each store stocks one thousand items. The chain must keep track then of the inventory of three hundred thousand items from a total of three hundred stores. This tracking must be performed on a daily basis.

Some chains solve this problem by using special sales registers that hook up to a computer in back of the store.

As a sale is made, the salesperson enters an inventory descriptor to identify the item and the price. This information is accumulated by the back office computer which subtracts the item from its inventory list and adds the price paid to its receipts list. The back office computer maintains these totals and can prepare a summary for the store's management. In addition, the single store computer transmits its information via the telephone lines to a larger computer system at regional headquarters. The regional system will prepare summaries and totals for the region and transmit its information to the national headquarters computer.

The chain of command is from the distributed small computers at the local branch, through the larger system at regional headquarters, and finally to the still larger system at national headquarters. To stress the hierarchical nature of this distributed system we described each system from local to national as larger than the other. This is not necessary, all computers could be small computers or one could use a different combination of small and medium systems. The essential point to remember is that computer power was distributed throughout the organization and computers have the ability to "talk" to each other.

4

Memory

Do you know your social security number? This is one of the most important individual designations in use today. We must record our social security numbers on our income tax statements, our medical insurance forms, our bank account applications, and a variety of other application forms too numerous to mention. Try polling the people around you to see if they remember their social security number. You'll find that most people haven't the slightest idea of the numbers that make up this most important descriptor.

While few people know their social security number, even fewer people are concerned at this general lack of memory. In fact, there's no cause for alarm. When asked to record this magic number on one of the many forms, we simply remove our social security card from our wallets and read the number. So while the number is not imbedded in our conscious memory, it is easily procured by reference to another medium.

There are some people who steadfastly avoid cluttering

Photographs obtained courtesy of Digital Equipment Corporation.

2. Computer System (magnetic disk pack highlighted)

their mind with facts. Their approach is to refer to the various directories, encyclopedias, dictionaries, and other reference and text books. While this approach frees their minds for more profound thinking, if carried too far, they will wind up spending too much of their time looking up information.

We must strike a proper balance between cluttering our memory banks with trivial information and economizing our time by avoiding excessive waste in searching for information. The difference, however, between important and trivial information is entirely up to the individual's discretion. Some people find life to be more enjoyable if they can name the date that Babe Ruth hit his sixtieth home run, others the date that Columbus made his second voyage to the New World.

The point is that memory is not just remembering. We all use selectivity in the memory process. Memory is more than remembering facts; it is also remembering where you can find the facts.

Whether they are aware of it or not, everyone uses some sort of organizational hierarchy for storing information. Depending on the value of the information and the speed with which we want to retrieve it, we store the information in a variety of media. The medium with the largest storage density and fastest information retrieval capability is also the least understood. It's the human memory. Other storage media that you've probably used is paper for writing notes, photographs for visual remembrances, and dictaphone tapes for the spoken word. The American Indian used the wooden totem pole, ancient Mayans recorded their memories in stone.

The various storage selections you make are not limited to information. You regularly solve your "things" storage problems, what to do with the skis, boots, and heavy jackets when winter is over, where to store cancelled checks and bills so they're available when income tax time comes around, etc.

Here again is a situation in which you want to avoid clutter. Unlike information storage where the valuable storage medium is your brain's memory, the valuable storage medium to remain uncluttered is your living space; the kitchen, the bedroom, living room, etc.

People dealing with computers are faced with comparable decisions about the type of storage media to use and the specific type of information to store on each type of medium. Computers do not have unlimited storage. As a result, a user must decide which information will permanently reside within the computer and which information will reside outside until the information is ready to be entered. For the information that will reside outside the computer, the programmer must select the storage medium. For both kinds of information, there must be a scheme for easy access.

Successful computer operation requires a proper balance between the cost of memory, the storage capacity, and the speed of accessing the information stored. As computer designers discovered approaches toward providing the optimum balance, they also invented a variety of different memory storage media and devices.

Main Memory and Auxiliary Memory

In spite of all the major technical advances that have occurred in the computer's development, its memory capacity still has an upper bound. Over the years manufacturers have designed different types of memories with increasing capacities. However, computer memory still consists of the main memory portion and the auxiliary (or standby) portion.

To explain this memory distinction, let's look at the

human memory process and then we'll see how it applies to computer memory.

The human memory is located within the brain. Information is stored and retrieved. When you introduce yourself to another person, you are accessing the information stored within your brain that tells you your name. This process is performed almost instantaneously. In fact it's so automatic that we're not even aware it's taking place.

For the human being we can say that the brain is the main memory. The brain has a large capacity and information can be accessed and retrieved quickly. Almost all of our daily activity is controlled by the information stored within our main memory or brain.

We have already mentioned that even the brain has a limited capacity and as a result, we are required to use other sources of memory storage. If you are introduced to ten people, you probably will not remember each individual's name. Perhaps you will write each name on a sheet of paper and alongside each name some brief description of each individual. You can then introduce anyone of these ten people to another person by referring to the notes on your sheet of paper. The sheet of paper serves the function of auxiliary memory for this situation.

Let's focus in on the process. You read the information from the auxiliary storage (sheet of paper). The information is transferred to your main memory (brain memory). Your mental processing unit (brain) then accesses the information from your brain memory and directs your body to act accordingly.

Continuing with the introduction analogy, if you were required to introduce these ten people twenty times per hour, you can see that reference to the sheet of paper would be tedious and time consuming. Instead, you will "memorize" the ten names. In computer terminology, you transferred the information from auxiliary memory to main memory.

If after one week these ten individuals leave and you hardly ever see them again, you will probably forget their names. This is not a problem since you have no need to remember their names. However, if at some future time you must recall the names, you can refer to the sheet of paper (provided of course you saved the listing). In computer terminology, you have erased the information from main memory.

We have already said that it makes sense to "memorize" the list of names if you are introducing the individuals at the rate of twenty introductions per hour. Obviously, if you only have to introduce these individuals once every two years, it would not be worthwhile to memorize the list of names. A question that comes to mind is for how many introductions does it make sense to memorize the list? Clearly, the answer depends on the individual performing the introductions and the circumstances involved in the introductions. We cannot and indeed should not give a definite answer.

In the same vein, the question of when to transfer information residing in a computer's auxiliary memory for semi-permanent residence in its main memory depends on the particular circumstances. However, in both cases a strong dosage of common sense will go a long way toward arriving at a good solution.

Another question to ask is, how long a time should the information be stored in main memory? The information should be stored in main memory only as long as it's needed. Here again, however, for both the human and the computer, common sense must rule since, in many cases you will not be able to predict this exactly. For example, perhaps the ten individuals visit sporadically. Should you always have their names in your memory? Can you always remember their names even if you wanted to?

In the example under discussion, a sheet of paper is the auxiliary storage medium. However, what if the room is too dark to read the names? Under such conditions the paper is a poor medium, perhaps a recorded message on a dictaphone would be better. Here again, we want to emphasize that the specific medium used also depends on the particular circumstances; whether it's paper, stone, film, etc.

Memory Architecture

Leaving price aside, the two major features of concern in selecting memory types are capacity (how much information can be held), and access speed (how quickly the stored information can be located). Figure 4.1 illustrates four different types of memory architecture. As you'll see, you're already familiar with these types of memories from your non-computer experience.

To help the discussion, let's say some piece of information is stored on each of the memories illustrated. Perhaps the piece of information is the name and telephone number of your lawyer. The object is to retrieve this data from the memories illustrated in Figure 4.1.

Pigeon Hole: The pigeon hole type of memory is the term which denotes the arrangement of storage compartments similar to those used by the postal service for postal boxes. It is also one of the favorite type of mailbox systems of schools for teachers' mail.

Assume the information we want is located in box B3 as indicated by the X. To access and retrieve the information, one simply goes directly to the appropriate hole and removes the information. Note that the access is direct, there is no waiting. After the information at X is accessed, it's just as easy to get the information at Y. We'll see later how this type of computer memory is used for main memory. When the various pigeon holes are accessed electronically, the data is immediately accessed.

FIGURE 4.1

TYPES OF MEMORY ARCHITECTURE

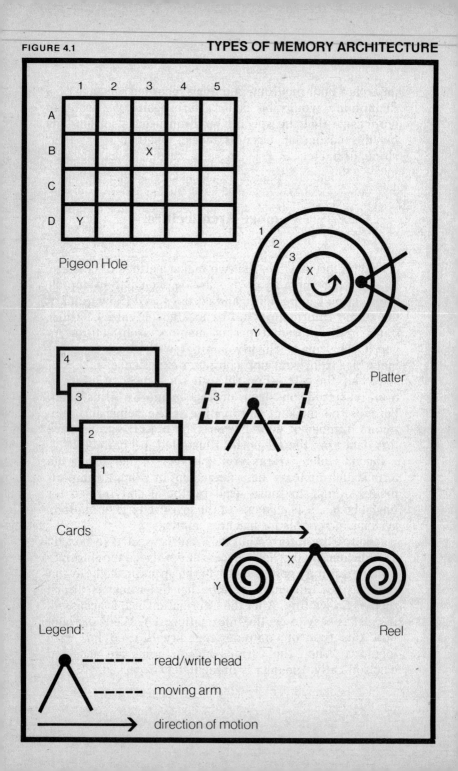

Platter: The platter type of memory is similar to a phonograph record. Instead of grooves, however, consider that the surface is covered with circular tracks. The platter memory utilizes an arm that contains a head for reading the data. The platter mechanism requires two moving parts. First, the reading head must be placed over the appropriate track. Second, the platter must spin around until the information on the appropriate track comes under the head.

Assume the information we want is at location X on track number 3. The information retrieval process involves moving the arm to track number 3 and waiting for the platter to spin the information under the head. If after getting the information at X, one wants the information at position Y (track number 1), the same arm and platter motion is required. You can go to X as quickly as you can go to Y, and on the average you can move from any point on the platter's surface to any other point just as quickly.

Reel: You're probably familiar with the tape reel from a hi-fi set or tape recorder. Information is recorded on a long strip that wraps around a reel. The strip is unwound from one end while the other end wraps around the takeup reel. With this system, the reading head is stationary and only the strip moves.

Unlike the pigeon hole and platter types of memory, the usefulness of the reel type of memory depends to a great extent on the sequence with which the information is accessed. To access the information at point X, the reel will turn and the strip will move until the information reaches the stationary head. The information at point Y can be accessed in the same way. Recall that with the pigeon hole and platter types it's just as fast to access first point X then point Y as it is to access the sequence Y then X. However, with the reel type, see what happens if you want to access first Y then X. The strip will move point X past the head without any reading taking place since information at point Y is required first. The strip will also

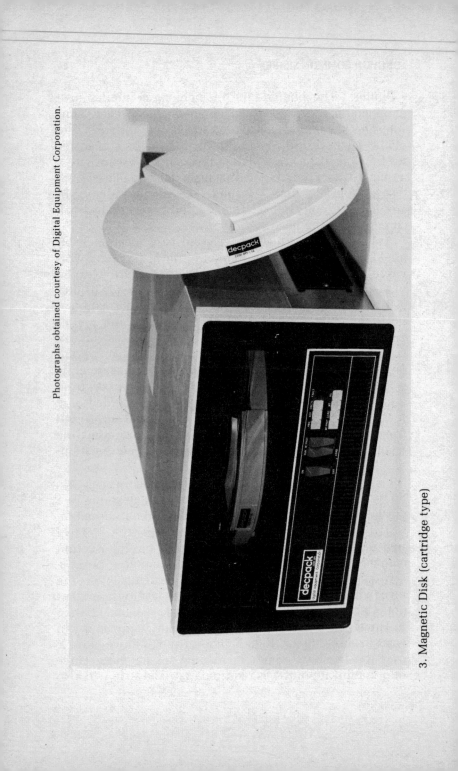

Photographs obtained courtesy of Digital Equipment Corporation.

3. Magnetic Disk (cartridge type)

move the complete distance from point X to point Y until Y is over the read head. After Y is read, the strip must move backward until X is over the head. The distance from X to Y had to be traversed twice for the sequence Y then X, while it had to be traversed only once for the sequence X to Y.

The platter or pigeon hole memory works just as well even if the information is not arranged in any particular order or sequence. Because of this characteristic, these memories are frequently called "random access memories." With the reel type of memory, it's important to consider the sequential order in which the information will be accessed. For example, if the reel memory stores a list of names and you want to access these names in alphabetical order, you must store the names in alphabetical order. Otherwise, your accessing time will be unnecessarily long while waiting for the strip to move back and forth.

Cards: Index cards and file folders are a very familiar form of storage in most business offices. Information is recorded on the cards and the cards are arranged in some alphabetical or numerical order. At least two motions are involved with cards. First, the arm (usually finger) moves along the deck to locate the card of interest. Second the card is removed from the deck and the information is read.

If the deck of cards is on a carousel device, the card can be returned after the information is read. With a carousel arrangement, any point is accessed as easily as any other, and sequencing of information is comparable to the platter. As a result, cards on a carousel can be considered random access memory.

If the card is maintained as a solid deck, it will be difficult to replace the extracted card. In this case, as each card is thumbed through it is placed in a bin. After all information is accessed, the deck is put together. Once a card is placed in an output bin, it cannot be conveniently accessed as in the case of the carousel. For this situation, then, the sequence of information is extremely important. Indeed sequencing is even more important than in the case of reel memory, and, not surprisingly, this would represent a case of sequential memory.

The Medium and the Message

While we discussed the various mechanisms used for organizing and storing information, we will now consider the specific media used for its actual recording.

The tape system in a hi-fi set uses a magnetic coating medium. Information is stored in the form of microscopic magnets, with each portion having a different strength. The magnetic forces are converted into electrical signals and in turn when these signals are passed through the system's electronics they produce sound from the loudspeaker.

Paper can also serve as a medium. The ancients used scrolls for recording events as well as depicting illustrations. To access a specific piece of information, the user unrolls the scroll. The ticker tape for stock quotations is another form of written words on paper in a reel type mechanism. In this case the information is stored as words on paper. The human reads the information directly in these cases. However, the information could also be read by a modern optical character reader.

Another medium for storing information can be empty holes punched in a tape or card. The holes are arranged according to a predefined code, perhaps two holes represent the letter B, three the letter C, etc. These are the computer cards you receive as bills with the familiar request, "Do not fold, spindle, or mutilate." A coating of semiconducting material can also be used as the medium.

For this case the information would be stored as different electrical charges.

The light reflecting properties of materials can also be changed. In this case, the information would be stored by different reflection intensities, different colors, or a variety of different optical characteristics that we need not discuss here.

Each year, new advances in the understanding of material structure give rise to potential new forms of memory media. Some of these excite the "memory makers," and generate considerable publicity, then they never appear in the marketplace for a variety of reasons. However, every few years a new type of memory medium proves itself and does gain market acceptance.

Bits and Bytes

As we've mentioned, all the information moving around within the computer's circuits stems from electrical and magnetic signals. Clearly, these systems need some sort of code to decipher the signals.

Most schoolchildren learn about Samuel Morse and his invention of the telegraph. Along with his telegraph, he also invented a system of codes. The Morse code is the familiar system of dots and dashes we used to read about in the spy novels. The dot was a short click, while the dash was a long bleep. The beginning of Beethoven's Fifth Symphony begins DOT DOT DOT DASH! This series of notes also happens to be the Morse code for the letter V. During World War II, Germany's opponents frequently broadcasted these notes to their citizens, as well as to the occupied countries, to boost morale. This V for VICTORY was a familiar slogan during that time. Here's a case where just two sound intervals, one short, one long, had an effect on multitudes of individuals and played a role that transcended their original, fairly mundane technological purpose. One can express quite a lot of information with just two sounds.

During the invention of the computer, the dot-dash terminology could have been adopted. It might have made understanding computer language simpler, since many people were already comfortable with the telegraph code terminology. But we live in an age where everyone looks for the catchy phrase. Perhaps we're concerned that people won't think it's new if we give the new invention a familiar name.

In the case of the computer, the dots and dashes are not short and long sounds. The computer dots when a memory element is magnetized in one direction (for magnetic media) or electrically charged positive (for semiconductor media). The computer dashes when the memory element's magnetization is reversed or electrically oppositely charged. In the case of the Morse code and the computer code we're dealing with a two-state situation; long/short, charged positive/charged negative, up/down, in/out, magnet up/magnet down, big/small, full/empty, etc.

Two is a nice concept. There's "tea for two," "cocktails for two," the two-step dance, two people in love, and a host of beautifully poetic references to "two." Unfortunately, when they invented the computer they were apparently too busy for poetry. A contemporary technologist would refer to each of the above as a binary tea, a binary cocktail, a binary step dance, and a binary love situation.

"Binary" is the high class word that refers to a thing or situation that has two parts. In a computer memory the "thing" that has two parts is called a "bit" (short for binary digit). The physical manifestation of the bit depends on the nature of the memory medium. For a magnetic medium the bit is a microscopically small area that's magnetized in one direction or another. For a paper computer card, the bit is a small area of the paper that has a hole or does not have a hole.

Since, in the final analysis, a human being is using the information processed by the computer, computer code should relate to something a human will understand. We can understand words and numbers. So just as the various dots and dashes of Morse code represent the letters of the alphabet and the digits one through nine and zero, we are not surprised to see a similar relationship for bits.

Think of each bit as a dot if it is magnetized up, charged positively, etc. and as a dash for the respective down and negative states. Now, how many different digits can two bits represent? Let's see:

        dot dot   =   1

        dot dash   =   2

        dash dot   =   3

        dash dash =   4

We've used up all the combinations available for two bits. It turns out that three bits will allow eight combinations for a corresponding eight digits, but that's not enough to represent the ten numerical digits and twenty-six letters of the English alphabet. That representation requires thirty-six combinations. Well, four bits will only provide sixteen combinations and five bits give thirty-two combinations—still four short. Six bits will provide sixty-four combinations, so we can use combinations of six bits to represent the numbers and letters and still have thirty-two combinations left over for other things. What other things?

When you look at a typewriter keyboard, you will notice it has a comma, a dollar sign, a quotation mark, and other special characters. In addition, an upper case A requires a different code from a lower case a. If we want the computer code to have at least the same flexibility provided by a typewriter, we need more than the thirty-two combinations we originally mentioned. When we include the typewriter's backspace key, the carriage return, and other similar features, we arrive at a figure of about one hundred different combinations. So since six bits only offer sixty-four combinations, it is not the most ideal number of bits to use.

Seven bits will provide one hundred twenty-eight combinations. Apparently seven bits should be sufficient. However, for a variety of technical reasons, it's best to use an even number of bits, so eight bits is the magic number that has evolved for representing alphanumerics by combinations of bits.

The group of eight bits is called a "byte."

In general, computer manufacturers have standardized their system's codes to conform to the byte concept. For your purposes, you can consider each byte as a character. For example, the word "cat" has three letters; it would be represented by three bytes (one byte for each letter). Since we are dealing with letters and numbers, it's more general to speak of characters. So to write the name of secret agent "31BOY" would require five bytes since the name has two digits (31) and three letters (boy).

When you speak to a salesperson in a personal computer store, or if you find yourself at a meeting of personal computer enthusiasts, you may hear the terms "kay bytes," "kay bits," or various other "kay" nouns. Sometimes, you may hear that "kay" has been replaced by "mega." Who is "kay" and what is "mega"?

Because memory storage capacities are large, on the order of thousands or millions of bytes, computer terminology adopts the scientific shorthand of these large quantities. "Kilo" equals thousand; "mega" equals million. As a result, storage capacities are usually quoted as kilobytes or megabytes. A further step in the shorthand is to refer to Kbytes or

Mbytes, respectively. The term "Kbytes" is frequently pronounced "kaybytes." The term "Mbytes" is usually pronounced "megabytes."

Storage Sizes

Quoted storage sizes for memories can sometimes be misinterpreted. Let's see how you can calculate the minimum storage capacity for a simple situation and we'll generalize from there.

Assume you want to store payroll information for fifty employees. Perhaps the information to be stored is the following:

Information Element	Number of Characters
Employee Name	30 (we must leave space for long names)
Salary	9 (e.g. $20000.65)
Social Security Number	11 (e.g. 185-29-2051)
Date	8 (e.g. 11/29/78)
Total	58

Obviously there could be much more information stored, such as home address if the check is mailed to the employee, the expense code to which the salary is charged, etc. However, we want to keep the example simple to get a specific point across. Each employee's payroll information will occupy at least 58 characters of basic information. Since one character equals one byte, it is obvious that at least 58 bytes of memory will be occupied by each employee's information. Since one byte equals eight bits, the storage occupied will be 464 bits for each employee.

In addition to the storage required for the actual data in the employee's record, the system requires some housekeeping designators so it can distinguish between the different types of information elements. For example, the system must be told that $20000.65 is the salary and as a result, it can perform the proper operations on this element of data. We do not want to get into the housekeeping details. However, we can roughly estimate that the housekeeping information will add about ten percent to the character count. Consequently, the employee record we've been discussing will occupy about 64 bytes or 512 bits. Since there are fifty employees, the storage required will occupy 3200 bytes (3.2 Kbytes) or 25,600 bits (25.6 Kbits).

If the same payroll information were processed manually without the aid of a computer, the group of information elements (name, salary, etc.) that describe each employee would be called a "record." The "records" **for** the complete staff of fifty employees would be called the "employee file." Computer people employ the same terminology.

A "record" is the collection of data and information that describes and characterizes the item under consideration.

A "file" is a collection of associated records.

In reference to the payroll file, we would say that the employee record requires 64 bytes of storage, while the complete file requires 3.2 Kbytes of storage. To get an estimate of the storage space required by any file, use the following procedure.

- 0 Determine the number of characters required for each information element in the record. Be sure to plan ahead. Leave room for the longest name or identifier that may come down the pike.
- 0 Add the number of characters for each information element. This will be the total number of characters for each record.

0 Multiply the number of characters by 1.1 (e.g. 1.1 times 58 equals 64). This number is the amount of computer storage that each record will occupy multiply the amount of computer storage per record by the number of records in the file. This number is the amount of computer storage (in bytes) that the file will occupy.

0 If you need to know how many bits the file will occupy, multiply the previous number by eight, since eight bits make one byte.

Core Storage

Core storage is used for main computer memory. It is directly connected to the central processor. Core storage gets its name from the fact that it's composed of tiny magnetic doughnuts (cores) strung together by wires (see Figure 4.2).

The principle of core storage's operation is the fact that when an electrical current is sent through a wire, the current also produces a magnetic field in the space outside the wire. This magnetic field interacts with the magnetic field of the core and causes a change in the core's magnetization. In computer memories, the change produced by the electric current's wire is to reverse the core's direction of magnetization (clockwise to counterclockwise as in Figure 4.2). While the direction does not actually change from up to down (or vice versa), it's convenient to speak in these terms. The important point is that the magnetic core is a two-state (or binary) element. The "states" are magnetization in one direction and magnetization in the opposite direction. To simplify the terminology, computer people speak of the up direction and down direction. They could just as well have spoken of East/West, North/South, in/out, over/under, or

FIGURE 4.2

CORE STORAGE

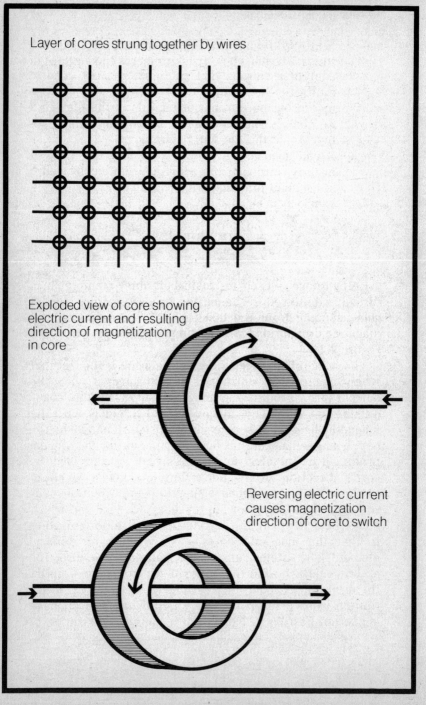

Layer of cores strung together by wires

Exploded view of core showing electric current and resulting direction of magnetization in core

Reversing electric current causes magnetization direction of core to switch

any other of a variety of opposites. However, the plain fact is that they speak of up/down. Sometimes they characterize the states in mathematical terminology as 1/0.

Core storage is an example of "pigeon hole" storage. Each core is a bit and can be accessed electronically at electronic speeds. There are no moving parts to slow up data access or data transfer.

Through the years, core storage data access speeds have increased from millionths of a second to billionths of a second. One billionth of a second is called a nanosecond. So while computer people formerly spoke of microsecond access times, they are now speaking in terms of nanoseconds.

Core storage is the fastest storage, but it's also the most expensive. The high cost of core storage stems from the fact that each core must be threaded by a thin wire. This fabrication technique is costly. As a result, it is economically unfeasible to construct a computer system entirely from core storage.

Core storage is also permanent storage. The direction of magnetization will change only if a current is passed. As a result, when the computer is not in use, each core will retain its magnetization. In other words the core memory remembers the information even if the plug is pulled.

Each core can be as easily accessed as any other. In addition, the order in which any core is accessed does not affect the access time. In other words, core storage is direct access memory and will perform equally as well whether dealing with data that's arranged in a sequential or random fashion.

Semiconductor Memory

When it was originally developed, semiconductor memory was used for auxiliary storage such that data

Photographs obtained courtesy of Digital Equipment Corporation.

4. Magnetic Tape (reel type)

transfers from auxiliary memory to main memory and then to the central processor. While there are a variety of reasons for semiconductor memory's original use as auxiliary storage, perhaps the primary reason was lack of confidence. It was a new type of memory and users were more comfortable with core storage. However, semiconductor memory made significant inroads, and is now an accepted type of main memory.

Semiconductor memory stores information in the form of electrical charges. Instead of magnetic cores, think of electric batteries with their terminals charged plus and minus. Each plus/minus charge pair is a bit. The state of the bit can be changed by reversing the charge. For example, if terminal A is charged plus and terminal B is charged minus, a change of state would be making terminal A minus and terminal B plus. Symbolically, we can describe this change of state as going from plus/minus to minus/plus.

Unlike core memory which is made up of actual magnetic cores, semiconductor memory is not composed from tiny little batteries. Semiconductor memory is made by depositing materials with special electrical properties on suitable substrates. Without going too deeply into the construction details, let us mention that they involve the new microelectronic technologies that you've probably been hearing about in advertisements of pocket calculators.

All semiconductor materials continually undergo significant price decreases as manufacturers have developed better and more economical fabrication techniques. As a result, semiconductor memory is bit for bit considerably less expensive than core memory. In addition, since it's in the microelectronic realm, semiconductor memories also pack considerably more bits in the same volume. It's semiconductor memory that led to the introduction of low cost digital watches and pocket calculators.

Semiconductor memory has many of the characteristics of core memory. It is direct access memory and so will operate just as efficiently with sequentially or randomly arranged data. Semiconductor memory accesses information as quickly as core memory since it has no moving parts and all data transfers occur at electronic speeds.

One disadvantage of semiconductor memory is its "volatility." Whereas core will remember the data stored even if the plug is pulled, semiconductor memory will forget. Semiconductor memory requires a constant voltage to retain its information. In many cases, the volatility of semiconductor memory is unimportant since there are procedures for reloading information even though the plug was pulled and the memory erased. In addition, various backup systems have been developed for maintaining the voltage in case of emergency. For certain applications where split second monitoring is required the volatility factor can rule out the use of semiconductor memory. However, for the immediate future, semiconductor memory will be the primary computer main memory medium.

Magnetic Tape

Magnetic tape memory is available as reels, cartridges, or cassettes. They look very much like their counterparts you're familiar with from your hi-fi system. Magnetic tape is used for auxiliary storage. While reel, cartridge, or cassette operate in essentially the same manner, each specific type offers somewhat different capacity, price, and ease of loading.

The basis of magnetic tape memory is a thin coating of magnetic material on a plastic strip. The surface of the tape is divided into microscopic portions. Each portion is a bit. The bit is magnetized in one direction or another. Information is written on to the tape and read from the tape by a magnetic head. The tape passes by the magnetic head while it is winding and unwinding.

Unlike core and semiconductor memory, magnetic tape memory does have moving parts. It is a fact of life that electronic speeds are considerably faster than mechanical speeds. As a result, memory devices with moving parts have longer access times than electronic memories. Moving memories can usually access the required data in a few thousandths of a second (one thousandth of a second equals one milisecond). While a milisecond access time appears fast, when compared to the microsecond and nanosecond access times of electronic memory, it's slow. In fact, access times of moving memories are about one thousand to one million times slower than electronic memories.

For proper use of magnetic tape systems it's essential that the information be sequentially organized. If your file will be a directory of names and addresses in which names will be accessed alphabetically, then the names must be recorded in alphabetical order. But note this important feature. You cannot conveniently use the same tape file to access the information alphabetically by city of residence. If Adams, Hart, and Williams live in Altoona, what will happen? The tape will begin at the "A" section for Adams, move through Hart and end up at the "W" section for Williams. This excursion could use as much as one hundred feet of tape. Now if the next city is Boston and its residents are Arthur, Henry, and Washington, the tape must rewind the one hundred feet to return to the "A" section for Arthur. This rewinding process may take a few miliseconds, but it represents thousands of central processor cycles that are idle while the tape is moving back and forth.

One major advantage of magnetic tape memory is its compact shelf storage capability. The reel, cartridge, or cassette is removable. Just as you can have an extensive music library comprised from your hi-fi tapes, so the

computer user can store magnetic tape recorded data files
and programs in cabinets. This feature gives magnetic
tape memories virtually unlimited storage capabilities.
However, bear in mind that the storage is "off-line" on
reels housed in a cabinet. In order to bring the information "on-line" the tape must be mounted on the magnetic
tape system. This procedure does take some time to
accomplish. Whether it requires too much time will
depend on the application and the computer's workload.

Magnetic tape's off-line storage capability provides an
extemely useful security capability. In many installations, all the computer's files are read onto a magnetic
tape at the end of each day (computer people say the file
is "dumped" onto the magnetic tape). This is an insurance procedure. There have been numerous cases in
which the electrical power fails, or someone spills a cup
of coffee on the computer, or someone maliciously tries
to otherwise interfere with the computer's operation.
When such an event occurs, the data in the computer can
be lost or seriously changed. A company can lose its
entire customer file or its entire accounts payable file
under such circumstances. The business can be de-
stroyed. However, this will be avoided if the file is
recorded on a magnetic tape stored in a safe place. The
tape can be reloaded and the file reconstructed up to the
point at which the tape dump was made. While it's still
possible that the current day's information will be lost, at
least the loss will be minimized. In most cases the current
day's information can be reconstructed.

Another level of security is gained by storing the tapes
in a physically different location. This procedure will
guard against losing information due to fire. In fact some
companies store their important data files in caves so
they will be secure even against nuclear attack. The
information will be available for the files to be reconstructed. Unfortunately, they haven't yet figured out
who's going to be around to load the tapes.

While the reel, cartridge, and cassette function in essentially the same manner, it will be worthwhile to discuss them in a little more detail to learn something about their distinguishing characteristics.

Reel   The reel is the original form of magnetic tape storage. A reel consists of about 2400 feet of tape. The tape is one-half inch wide. Storage capacity is measured in terms of "packing density," which is the number of bytes packed into one linear inch of tape. Standard tape packing densities are 800, 1600, 3200, and 6400 bytes per inch. The higher the packing density, the more data that can be stored on a single reel. Designers are constantly striving to increase the packing density. Reels are loaded onto the magnetic tape system by threading one end through a slot and attaching it to a so-called rewind reel.

Cartridge   Cartridge is virtually identical to reel tapes. However, the cartridge is much easier to load. It requires no threading of tape. The user simply snaps the cartridge onto the magnetic tape system. It is similar to the difference between loading reel-to-reel tape and eight-track tape cartridges for your hi-fi system.

Cassette In the realm of the personal computer, cassettes are among the primary auxiliary storage units. Most users are familiar with these devices and already have them for their audio applications. Usually, a fairly inexpensive interfacing control unit will enable cassette players/recorders to operate with most personal computer processors. In addition, a considerable volume of independent software is offered on cassettes. During a stroll through Ruth Janet's Platter Palace, you will find almost as many cassette tapes covering such subjects as payroll, inventory control, and accounts receivable as classical or country/western music. Indeed, perhaps the largest number may be Space Battles, Return of Conga, and a bewildering variety of exotic computer games.

In general, as with their hi-fi counterparts, cassette tapes are less expensive than their reel and cartridge counterparts. In addition, cassette tapes have smaller dimensions and, as a result, hold less data. However, the cassettes' smallness and comparatively low cost are what make them particularly attractive. Cassette equipment is compact; a standard sized desk typewriter can have a built-in magnetic cassette without affecting its size. With such a setup, the information can be captured as computerized signals on magnetic tape while the typist is typing, as well as on hard copy paper as is done with a standard typewriter. Tape cassettes can be easily transported through the mails to avoid telephone communications transmission costs (providing the time element is not crucial).

Magnetic Disk Systems

Magnetic disk systems furnish auxiliary storage. They are analogous to phonograph records. The platter or disk is coated with a magnetic film which is divided into microscopic portions. Each portion is a bit.

Because the platter spins on its axis, the bits are arranged as concentric circles (see Figure 4.3). Each circle is called a "track." A read/write head connected to an "arm" reads data from the tracks and writes data onto the track. Magnetic disks generally require a two-step process for accessing data. First the arm must move over the track that contains the data item. Second the system must wait until the data item on the track reaches the read/write head. Since data access requires mechanical motion, disk access times are considerably slower than those for core and semiconductor memory. Typically, disk access times are in the milisecond range (a milisecond equals a thousandth of a second).

Designers have come up with a variety of approaches to reduce data access times. In the "fixed-head disk" movement of the arm to the selected track is avoided by permanently placing a reading head over the surface of each track. If a platter has one hundred tracks, there will

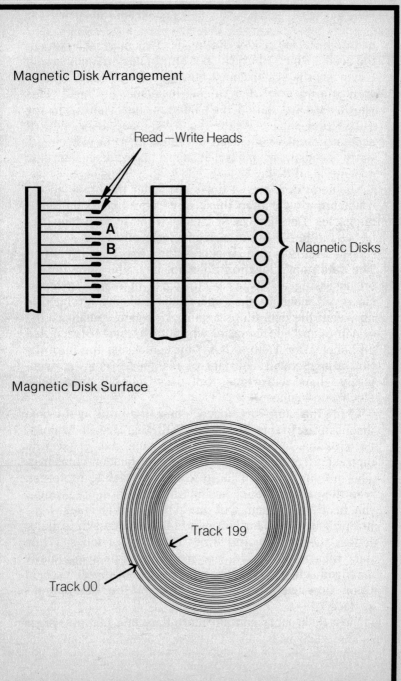

Magnetic Disk Arrangement

Read–Write Heads

A

B

Magnetic Disks

Magnetic Disk Surface

Track 199

Track 00

be one hundred read/write heads. This approach can cut the access time in half since it eliminates one movement. However, the system must still wait for the data item to spin around until it is under the read/write head. This waiting time is called the "latency time" and is in the milisecond range. While the fixed head disk reduces access time, it's construction requirement of many read/write heads also makes it more expensive than the moving head disk.

Magnetic disk access times are faster than tape access times but slower than those of core and semiconductor memories. Data is accessed more directly than tape, but not as randomly as for core and semiconductor.

Any data item can be accessed as easily as any other. The data item's location does not have the same impact on accessing ability as in the case of magnetic tapes. However, magnetic disk operating efficiency is related to how well the data file is organized. Again consider a list of names and addresses for which the names are recorded alphabetically. With a disk, you can access the information alphabetically by city of residence (more conveniently than with tape, but less quickly than with electronic memory).

Using the same directory we described during the tape discussion, Adams, Hart, and Williams live in Altoona. Perhaps the "A" section is on track one, the "H" section on track fifty, and the "W" section on track one hundred. The moving arm will jump from one track to the other, wait the proper latency period until the data comes under the head, and then will jump to another track. This jumping back and forth does add to the access time, but it is less than the rewind times required for tapes. While data files for disks are not required to be sequentially arranged, clearly, the operating efficiency will depend upon how well the data is laid out on the platter's surface.

Most disk packs contain more than one platter. Larger

storage capacity is achieved by stacking as many as ten platters and using the top and bottom surfaces for storage. This configuration furnishes twenty surfaces. Of course, each surface requires its own moving arm and read/write head mechanism.

Magnetic disks offer the same off-line storage capabilities as magnetic tapes. In most cases, the disk pack is removable. A library of disk packs can reside on a shelf; the user simply loads the appropriate disk when the stored information is required. In addition to unlimited off-line storage, magnetic disks also provide the same insurance features provided by magnetic tape. Important data can be periodically dumped onto a library disk that is stored in a different location from the main computer system. If anything happens that causes a loss of information, it can be reconstructed from the library disk.

Manufacturers offer a variety of disk systems. Some are fixed head for faster data access while others are removable. Some disk packs contain the moving arm mechanism, others contain only the platters while the moving arm mechanism is located in the disk drive's housing.

The "floppy disk" or "diskette" is one of the more recent disk systems and the one most closely associated with the personal computer. The magnetic disk counterpart of the magnetic tape cassette, it is a thin, flexible disk similar to a 45 rpm record. A blank diskette can cost about the same price (or perhaps 50 percent more) than a high-quality tape cassette cartridge. In contrast, so-called "hard" disk packs can cost as much as ten times the price of a diskette. Of course, the "hard" systems have much greater storage capacity.

In general, tape systems cost less than disks. One reason is that cassette tape recorders/players have been available to consumers for audio applications for many years. In fact, the diskette/tape cassette choice is one area where a distinction can be made between the hobby computer and the personal computer used for business. The hobbiest has limited funds and will usually elect for the tape cassette economy. In a business environment, however, the personal diskette computer system is more economically feasible. Usually, at least two diskette players/recorders are required (i.e., one plays while the other makes copies). Because diskette systems are more prevalent in business that in strictly home applications, most computer games are made available on tape cassettes rather than on diskettes.

Information on a floppy disk is recorded on one side and for protection the disk is usually permanently contained in an envelope of dimensions about eight inches on each side. The floppy disk is a low cost and compact system that rivals the cassette in its use. Just as cassette readers are now included as components of such devices as typewriters, many manufacturers are featuring floppy disk options. The disk is quite suited for the mails, simply place it in an envelope. In fact some governmental agencies will accept tax information completed on a floppy disk. The disk can be sent in place of a completed paper form. The recipient agency will load the disk onto its computer system to read the information making the reporting process simpler for both parties.

5

Typing In/Printing Out

We'll now discuss the human side of computing. In spite of all the complaints we hear about the computer replacing the human being, we are happy to report that the human is the most important component of any computer system. We humans write the programs that control the computer's processing; we provide the computer with all the data it needs to perform its calculations; we are the folks who take the computer's results and transform them into houses, machinery, highways, and pleasant parks where poets can sit beside shady trees and create verses that lament our technological age.

The communication between computer and humans is an extremely important part of any computer system. While there are a few computer system applications in which the computer and human communicate by speaking to each other, the most prevalent communication medium is through the written word. We inform the computer of our desires by typing information through an electronic keyboard; each key is connected to electric

Photographs obtained courtesy of Digital Equipment Corporation.

5. CRT Terminal

circuits that transform the characters into codes that the computer can understand. The computer in turn gives us results by printing reports that we can read. As we'll see later, there are many other devices that can be used to "type in and print out" from the computer. In fact, computer people speak of the general terms "input" and "output."

Devices used for getting information into a computer are called input devices. Those for getting information from a computer are called "output devices." Computer people group them together under the term "input/output" and frequently abbreviate the name to "I/O." We could have called this chapter "input/output," but "typing **in**/printing out" is a more descriptive and less formidable title. (Author's license in the interest of clarity should always be forgiven.)

Input/output devices fall into many categories. One important classification that has been found useful is the difference between "machine understandable" and "human understandable."

Human understandable input/output devices generate computer output in a form that is understandable to the human being (e.g. printed page, television screen, photograph, etc.). The same term is used for devices that enable the human to input information into the computer in a form understandable to the human (e.g. typewriter keyboard, handwritten notes, voice, etc.).

Humans cannot type or read as fast as computers can process. So one recurring problem with human understandable I/O devices is their relative slowness. The largest cost for running a computer installation is in the salaries and fringe benefits of the human programmers, operators, and managers. As a result, it makes economic sense to replace the human interface with automated input/output devices wherever possible. In addition such a policy frees up the human to perform even more vital functions for the organization.

Machine understandable input/output devices store information in a form that is readily transferred between themselves and computers. They operate at considerably faster speeds than do humans and can handle correspondingly more data in information transfers. Clearly, one problem with a strictly machine understandable I/O device is that the human cannot read the information it contains. This is overcome by employing other devices that convert from machine to human understandable formats.

In a previous chapter we discussed magnetic tapes and disks as they perform in the memory arena. However, all auxiliary storage devices can also be considered machine understandable input/output devices. We are not introducing a contradiction; auxiliary storage devices are multifunctional, depending upon how they're used.

As an example of how an auxiliary storage device can also be used as an input/output device, let's discuss one particular application for a floppy disk. Imagine that you want to send the same letter to fifty different individuals. Of course you can type the letter once and make fifty copies. But this will not give each letter a personal touch. If these are requests for a donation or a job, you'll probably want to personalize each letter. The recipient will be better disposed toward considering your request if he sees his name on the letter.

So now you're faced with typing fifty different letters. But the body of each letter will be identical, only the recipient's name and address will be different. Computerized "word processing" will give you a way around this problem. It will allow you to type the body of the letter just once. While we want to avoid too much detail, imagine a typewriter that also has a built-in floppy disk. As you type the body of the letter, the letter will be printed on the typewriter's paper medium. In addition, the information will also be stored on the floppy disk; you have also written the letter onto the floppy disk.

Now to create the fifty letters. Place a clean piece of paper in the typewriter. Type in the name and address of the recipient. Then press the button that activates the floppy disk. The disk will take control and type the letter. After the letter is completed, repeat the process for the remaining letters. Notice that the disk was an auxiliary storage medium when you typed the body of the letter. The disk became an input device when it took over control and typed the letter.

Although we used a floppy disk as an example, the same process is also performed by equipment consisting of a typewriter with a magnetic cassette instead of a disk. In fact, depending on the volume of work, there are other combinations of human and machine understandable devices that could be used.

Moving Is No Fun

Only a few years ago, you had to pay a few hundred dollars for the most accurate watches. In fact, their manufacturers called them timepieces and chronometers to add some class to the expense. Today you can get a digital watch even more accurate than these timepieces or chronometers for less than twenty dollars. The digital watch has no moving parts and can be fabricated by automated procedures. The chronometer had many moving parts. Despite the fact that many of its components were fabricated by automated procedures, they were still put together manually.

Most input/output devices operate with moving parts. They have little cogs and wheels that move paper, and activate a particular alphabetical key to turn a tape or disk, etc. The moving parts require exacting production techniques; they must be made with precision. While there have been considerable improvements in the man-

ufacture of input/output devices, their performances have
not improved in the same leaps and bounds as have the
performances of processors. Today you can purchase a
central processor for less than ten percent of the cost of a
1960 equivalent (and if we count inflation the cost is even
less). Prices for input/output devices have not decreased
as dramatically. However, with the improvements in
input/output devices, you do get more for your money
today than in the past. In addition, there are a variety of
lower priced input/output devices that are quite suitable
for many applications requiring less formidable capabilities.

Connection to Processor

Input/output devices attach to the central processor by
means of "data channels." A data channel is a piece of
hardware that regulates the flow of information so that
the processor is not overloaded with information and can
keep track of whose information is being processed at any
given moment. A data channel can attach more than one
input/output device to the central processor. In addition,
a central processor can have more than one data channel
attached. The specific numbers depend on the application and the manufacturer usually offers various capacity
data channels as options.

You must exercise some care when reading manufacturers' descriptions of data channel capabilities. As a
typical example, you may read that a particular computer
system can support eight separate data channels and that
each channel can itself carry sixteen input/output devices. Simple arithmetic tells you that the system can
support a total of one hundred twenty-four devices.
However, this may be an erroneous conclusion, since the

calculation tells you nothing about the performance of the channels; will the channel maintain the information flow of one hundred twenty-four devices operating simultaneously? In practically all cases the answer is no.

Think of the data channel information flow as comparable to an automobile highway system. In many large cities, the highway system contains several large cloverleaf intersections. Perhaps five to ten separate roadways converge at one point. When the traffic is not too busy (usually late at night during the week) there's no problem; all the traffic flows smoothly. However, during the rush hour when each roadway (or channel) is filled to capacity, the cloverleaf becomes a large bottleneck. Why does this happen? Because the cloverleaf itself has a limited capacity for handling traffic flow.

Say the cloverleaf can support a flow of five hundred cars per minute while each channel leading into the cloverleaf can support two hundred cars per minute. When the channels are loaded to capacity, the total of ten channels are sending two thousand cars per minute into a cloverleaf that can support only five hundred cars per minute; that's four times the capacity.

On the other hand, if two channels are loaded to capacity, while the remaining eight channels are empty, the cloverleaf will receive an input of four hundred cars per minute, well below its maximum capability of five hundred cars per minute. So under the proper circumstances the cloverleaf can support the traffic and avoid bottlenecks.

A similar situation will prevail with computer systems. Although a computer system is advertised as capable of supporting eight data channels, it probably can't support all eight operating simultaneously. More likely, only two or three can operate simultaneously. Similarly, while each data channel can support sixteen devices, only a small number of these devices can operate at the same time.

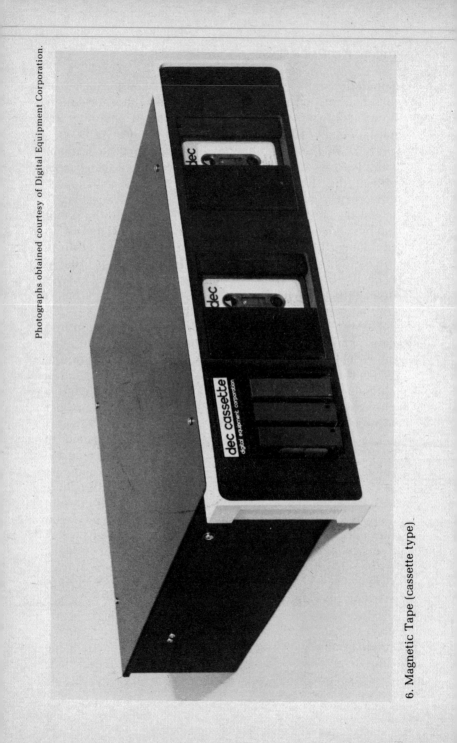

Photographs obtained courtesy of Digital Equipment Corporation.

6. Magnetic Tape (cassette type).

We don't want to get involved in heavy details of data speeds and dynamic capabilities. However, we do want to emphasize that with computers as with highways, the dynamics are significant. When you look at a highway road map, you're getting a static picture of the traffic pattern; ten converging roads can lead to a monumental traffic jam. Likewise, a computer system may have the static capability to hook up over one hundred devices, but they cannot operate at the same time.

When you consider a computer system, think of the processor as the highway cloverleaf. Find out the input/output data transfer speed of the central processor (usually quoted in terms of bytes per second). Next, determine the data transfer speeds of each channel and of each device on each channel. The total of the channel transfer speeds should be less than the processor's transfer capability. If the channel's load is greater, then analyze your application to determine whether each device must operate simultaneously. If they must operate simultaneously, then the system will be overloaded. However, in many cases, there can be non-simultaneous operations. As one example, consider a company that has terminals from each of the fifty states accessing its central computer system. While the computer may not be able to support simultaneous data flow from all fifty states, the problem can be overcome by limited access by each state to specific time periods. For example, California, Oregon, Washington can access during the hour 9 am to 10 am, while Florida, Georgia, Virginia can access from 10 am to 11 am.

Input/Output Devices

A wide range of input/output devices is currently available to the computer user. While they differ in capacity and performance, they are all designed to offer each user the best price performance break for his specific application.

Because the input/output device is also the point where the human and machine interact, the equipment is designed with considerable human engineering in mind. In the following we present descriptions of the major types of input/output devices. It's a safe bet to assume that most of the devices discussed come in a sufficiently wide range of performance and price characteristics such that you can find a device to fit your needs and budget. In addition, there are many cases where input/output systems consisting of combinations of devices are offered in the marketplace. Finally, if you are adventurous and don't see the device that would exactly fit your particular application, speak to a computer salesperson, they can usually direct you to a potential solution.

Serial Printers

Serial printers are devices that print one character at a time. They look like typewriters and include a keyboard for the operator to send input to the processor. As a result, serial printers generally provide both input and output capabilities. Some popular jargon terms for serial printers are Teletype and Selectric. These terms arise from the brand names of two major manufacturers. American Telegraph and Telephone manufactures the Teletype, and International Business Machines manufactures the Selectric. However, the marketplace contains many vendors of this type of equipment.

Serial printers are designed to operate in an "interactive mode." That is the user sits at one of these printers and talks to the computer by keying in data and instructions through the keyboard. The computer in turn responds by printing information on the paper placed in the printer. This type of interactive operation does not require very fast devices since the human can type and read only so fast. Serial printers will print at speeds of up to a few hundred characters per second, better than a human typist, but not really in the major leagues as far as computers go.

The serial printer is the standard input/output device used by most smaller installations and is also part of the input/output device complement of the larger systems. It offers hard copy printout in the form of typed characters on a paper page. This feature is usually employed for letter writing and other reports. If special forms are used, the serial printer can print checks, dinner menus, and almost anything else you can think of. However, the serial printer is usually limited to printing text, not graphics. It's inexpensive, reliable, and widely applicable.

CRT Display

The CRT display is used for input and output. CRT stands for cathode ray tube (your television set's picture tube is a CRT). CRTs are interactive devices, intended for the human user to communicate with the computer. The human enters information by means of a keyboard. The computer talks back by displaying information on the CRT screen.

As far as speed is concerned, the display need not be faster than the human can read and input is performed at speeds that humans can type. CRTs are competitors to serial printers. Both are designed for the same purpose, except that the CRT does not provide a hard paper copy. In some cases where you'll want hard copy, such as in your letter writing, the CRT is at a disadvantage while in other cases, such as in a parts inventory inquiry system where you may not want a hard paper copy, the CRT has its advantages. For situations where you might want CRT display and hard copy, you can get a combined system, consisting of a keyboard, a printer, and a CRT.

Many CRT devices provide graphic display capabilities that allow the display of circles and a variety of graphic plots. However, these "graphic" CRTs are more expensive than those which only display alphabetic and numeric characters.

Communicating Devices

Serial devices such as printers and CRTs are also used in portable communicating terminal devices. These terminals are lightweight and can be manufactured in a sufficiently durable fashion so they can accompany the traveler. The printers in particular look very similar to a portable typewriter. However, these terminals have one important added feature—they can talk to computers located as much as hundreds and even thousands of miles away. They communicate with computers by using the same vehicle that humans use to talk to each other from remote locations—the telephone network. This network is available to all users.

In order for a terminal to "speak" to a computer over ordinary telephone lines, it requires an "acoustic coupler" or "modem." This is necessary because computers use digital signals (e.g., ones and zeros, etc.) while the voice network uses "analogue" signaling (e.g., the carrier signal changes continuously and in direct proportion to the informational content variations). Basically, a transmitting terminal emits a digital signal, and the modem converts the digital signal into an analogue sound signal (e.g., a whistling sound of varying pitch). The analogue sound signal traverses the voice network until it reaches the modem of the destination computer. In a reverse process, the receiving modem converts the analogue voice signal into a digital signal that can be understood by the computer.

The technical term for the analogue to digital conversion process (and its reverse) is called modulation and demodulation, hence the term "modem." One form of modem that contributes to a terminal's portability is the "acoustic coupler." This device provides two receptacles that hold the speaking and listening ends of a telephone handset, respectively. As a result, terminals that include acoustic couplers can be used from public telephone booths, hotel rooms, etc.

Many personal computers are quite portable and lend themselves to traveling. Such a computer that includes an acoustic coupler can communicate with other personal computers, or more likely, with large, centrally located computer systems. Naturally, whether or not a communicating capability is required depends upon the application. It certainly is an unnecessary expense if it is a standard feature that you will never use. But as a capability for potential future addition, it can be an attractive option.

Line Printer

Line printers are strictly output devices. Unlike serial printers which print one character at a time, line printers churn out complete lines of text. Line printers spew out the familiar stacks of oversized green sheets commonly called "computer printouts."

Whereas a serial printer will print a few hundred lines during one minute of operation, a line printer can print several thousand lines in the same period of time. Indeed a line printer can produce more text in one minute than a human can intelligently read in one day.

Most of the output from line printers is never read by the same person. A typically productive use for a line printer is to produce payroll checks for a company's fifty thousand employees. For this type of application special forms will be used (sheets of paper with preprinted blank checks). Another application for a line printer is to produce a historical record of all computer activity. If some problem with the system develops, the output from the line printer can be investigated to search for the cause. As a general rule, only about twenty percent of the information stored on such line printer printout will ever be necessary. However, the computer user usually doesn't know in advance which twenty percent it will be. Consequently, line printers continue to churn out data and paper.

We don't want to give the impression that line printers are not useful. They are major components of all large computer installations and are necessary for generating large amounts of printed output in a short period of time. However, unless the line printer is used for the proper applications, it can be an inefficient and expensive paper eater. And always bear in mind; paper for line printers is not cheap.

We've already mentioned check printing and maintaining a historic file of computer operation as two good uses of line printers. Another use for line printers is to generate tables of financial information and produce printed drafts to use for checking spelling, grammar, and punctuation before printing reports in a more human oriented output format.

At their low speed range, line printers become cost competitive with serial printers. Since the slower speed line printers do operate faster than the higher speed serial printers, there's a range of applications where these two types of printers compete head on. Because of the wide range of price and speed combinations available, we cannot give you specific rules for selecting a serial or line

Photographs obtained courtesy of Digital Equipment Corporation.

7. Line Printer

printer for a particular application. However, one general guideline is to check to make sure that the printer you select can generate printed output at the same rate that the humans within your organization can make use of the information. An information glut caused by too much information can be just as bad (and in some cases worse) than an information shortage. In both cases valuable information will not be available when needed; in one case it's not there, in the other it's buried in so much garbage that the information becomes irretrievable.

As fast as the line printer can generate output, it is still considerably slower than the central processor. When a line printer is directly connected to the computer, situations can develop where the processor must interrupt processing while it is waiting for the line printer to print the data. To avoid this process interruption, the technique known as "spooling" was developed.

In "spooling," data intended for the line printer is first recorded on magnetic tape or disc. These magnetic media can record information in one continuous burst at much faster speeds than a line printer can print. This recording operation is "spooling." After the data is recorded, the tape or disk is removed.

The magnetic recording media is used in conjunction with a special "off line" line printer. The off-line printer is not directly connected to the computer. It consists of a magnetic tape or disk drive attached to a high speed printer. The disk or tape containing the spooled information is loaded on the corresponding off-line reader. As the tape or disk is played its data is printed by the line printer.

Line printers as well as serial printers perform the actual printing operation in a variety of ways. Two prevalent printing procedures are "impact" and "electrostatic."

"Impact printing" involves a key hitting the paper. The operation is quite similar to a regular typewriter, except that up to one hundred thirty keys comprising a single line hit the paper simultaneously (hence the term line printer). Another type of impact mechanism is the "matrix printer." Rather than a sculptured character impacting the paper, the matrix printer uses a mechanism that produces dots on the page; the dots form the shape of alphabetic and numeric characters. The matrix characters are produced in a fashion similar to many lighted advertising signs that also display messages. In most cases the dot pattern is sufficiently close so that it appears as a complete character to the naked eye.

One of the major features of impact printers that make them desirable is their ability to produce carbon copies. Up to six part paper is available to produce the original and five carbon copies for multiple distribution. While this is a benefit, the quality of the carbon copies can be degraded, particularly the higher order carbons.

"Electrostatic printing" involves a printing mechanism that produces sparks on a specially treated paper. This technique can be faster than impact mechanisms, but it requires the special paper and does not produce carbons. However, considering the quality of the carbons produced by impact printers, the electrostatic's lack of carbons may not be a problem.

Another type of printing operation that is becoming popular is the "xerographic" method. This produces excellent quality printed output and provides many of the positive features furnished by the familiar office copiers using this method. Two major manufacturers of these printers are Xerox Corporation and IBM.

Card Readers/Punches

The "punched card" has been around longer than even the computer. It was invented by Herman Hollerith for gathering and processing information during the 1890 census. However, with the advent of the computer, and in particular, computer billing to consumers, the punched card is now a familiar participant in our contemporary technological world. Among its many accomplishments has been to make each of us feel a little guilty whenever we "fold, staple, or mutilate."

As an output device the card punch actually punches holes in a card. The holes are punched according to a definite coding system understood by the computer. In addition to punching holes, the card punch can also print information on the card. As a result, punched card output is both machine and human readable.

For input, the computer reads the holes in the card and interprets the coding. In general, punched cards are both input and output devices. The same device can read the information from a card and punch information onto a card. However, there are applications where only one or the other operation is required. As a result, punched cards are input/output devices as well as just input and just output.

Punched cards are very popular for bill collecting. The customer receives a bill in the form of the punched card. Human readable information is printed on the card while the holes are machine readable. When the vendor receives the payment and the card, a simple human check is performed to verify the correct payment. Then the card can be fed into the computer for processing of the account.

Paper Tape Readers/Punches

Paper tape devices are input and output devices. Holes are punched in a paper or plastic tape. These devices are fast becoming outmoded since the introduction of the diskette and magnetic tape cassette. However, many paper tape devices are still in use and nostalgia as well as completeness dictates that a book about computers mentions them at least once.

Magnetic Tapes and Disks

We've already discussed magnetic tapes and disks from the auxiliary storage point of view. These devices operate in a similar manner when used for input/output. Because magnetic media is not human readable, tapes and disks serve as intermediary input/output devices primarily suited for quickly transferring information between different computers.

The low cost cassette and diskette versions of these input/output types are particularly suited for dedicated applications involving limited amounts of data such as letters and memos. Cassettes and diskettes are transportable via the mail for low cost transmission between distant locations.

We must mention one mixed media version of cassette and diskette systems that is gaining popularity. This is a combined printer with diskette or cassette. These systems consist of the keyboard and printer mechanism as well as a built in cassette or diskette drive. Data that's keyed in or printed out can simultaneously be captured on the diskette or cassette for later playback for computer input. As we mentioned in the discussion of auxiliary storage, these mixed media systems are particularly popular for word processing applications in an office environment.

MICR

MICR stands for Magnetic Ink Character Recognition and is primarily used in check processing applications within the banking industry. Take a look at the bottom portion of your personal checks. You'll see a series of numbers printed in a type style that's understandable, but at the same time is somewhat different from the ordinary type style you will see in books.

The ink used to imprint the characters contains magnetic particles. A computer can interpret the magnetic field set up by each character so that when it processes your check the computer automatically reads your account number. Even better, before your check is processed, an operator reads the dollar amount and types the value on the check using a special MICR printing device. With this procedure, the computer can read the account number, dollar amount, and other pertinent information such as the bank upon which the check is drawn.

Optical Readers

One goal of computer technologists is to have a device that enables the computer to read text in an unrestricted manner. While there are devices that can read particular forms of typed material under restrictive conditions, computers still cannot read manuscripts as easily as a human being. However, there have been many major advances worth discussing.

Optical readers are input only devices and come in two major categories; those that read and understand characters and those that read and understand a special bar code.

"Optical character readers" are usually referred to as OCR devices. They have the ability to scan a page of alphabetic and numeric characters and to interpret the images so that the shape of the letter "c" (for example) generates a code that is understood by the processor's

FIG. 5.1 EXAMPLE OF OBR PRINTING

This is an example of OBR printing. Note
the series of vertical lines below each
character. A human can understand the
characters, while an optical bar reader can
scan the vertical lines below each character
and convert them into signals that the
computer can understand.

logic. While this may appear to be a straightforward process, the OCR device requires considerable logic capabilities to achieve this result. Indeed all OCR devices must themselves incorporate a computer to perform this logic. As a result, OCR devices are usually expensive and limited in use to larger companies that have applications requiring conversion of large amounts of text to computer. However, most OCR devices are limited to reading only specific type styles under restrictive conditions. The day when inexpensive OCR devices will be capable of understanding hand written manuscripts is still a long way off.

"Optical Bar Readers" (commonly referred to as OBR devices) read a specially coded series of vertical bars. Each letter of the alphabet and number is represented by a distinct series of small vertical bars. The OBR device reads the bars and interprets the information. OBR input to computers is finding widespread use in billing applications. In a procedure similar to punched card billing activity, the vendor sends the customer a bill that also contains printed bar coded information. The customer returns the payment along with a portion of the original bill. After the payment is verified, the portion of the original bill is fed into an OBR reader for computer processing.

OBR code is strictly machine readable. However, most OBR printers combine this machine readable code with human readable letters and numbers. This combined machine/human capability is attained by using an arrangement whereby each character on a regular typewriter incorporates the optical bar code signal as well as the human readable character; the optical bar code usually appears directly under the printed character. As a result, each line can be read by a human as well as a computer; see Figure 5.1.

The logic required to decipher optical bar code is simpler than that required for understanding actual characters. Consequently, OBR devices are considerably less expensive and in more widespread use than OCR devices. OBR code has reached the supermarket. The series of strange looking lines that you will find in some corner of every package sold at the supermarket is an OBR code indicating the product identification and price. Many supermarkets and discount stores are obtaining special scanning devices that connect directly to the cash register at the checkout counter. In the old system the checkout clerk was required to read the price and key the numbers into a cash register. This procedure is slow and prone to errors. With the OBR system, the clerk scans the label and all the proper information is automatically read and fed into the computer in a single error free operation.

Voice Response

Like most humans, computers are better talkers than listeners. Actually, the computer itself is not doing the talking. Instead, the processor controls the operation of a tape recorded message. In more sophisticated systems, the recording consists of different phonetic sounds. A program in the computer controls the sequence of the sounds so that the human hears words, phrases, and sentences.

It's more difficult for the computer to understand a human voice because everyone speaks differently. However, investigators are experimenting with devices that can recognize a particular person's voice and respond to a series of simple commands such as stop, start, pause, etc.

Telephone Handset

The ordinary telephone is the most often used instrument having computer input capability. When you use the dial or the push button handset feature, you are sending coded information over the telephone lines. The information is interpreted by the telephone company's computer. Computer people take advantage of the handset's coding output capability to utilize the telephone as a computer input device. This activity is particularly popular with the push button devices. The ten numeric digits (zero and one to nine) are readily available and enable the user to input numeric information. In the near future, consumers will be communicating with computers via their telephone handset for such financial applications as paying bills by transferring money from a savings or checking account to the vendor's account, requesting the latest stock quotation by inputting the stock identifier and hearing a voice response for the answer, and a variety of other applications whose announcement simply awaits discovery by the host of clever people that make up our world.

Television

We're all familiar with the home video games that enable our families to play tennis, basketball, hockey, and a variety of other games on the television screen. The game playing attachments transform your television screen into a CRT screen similar to those used by input/output devices of the same name. Investigators are developing interfaces that will allow you to attach a keyboard with some microprocessor memory to your television set (or the keyboard will be the telephone handset). With this setup you'll have your own computer. We can look forward to the day when television commercials for cooking recipes are replaced by commercials for specialized programs (another type of recipe) to run your home television CRT display computer.

Micrographics

Micrographics is a general term for miniaturized photographic processes. Microfilm is one such process. It's

Photographs obtained courtesy of Digital Equipment Corporation.

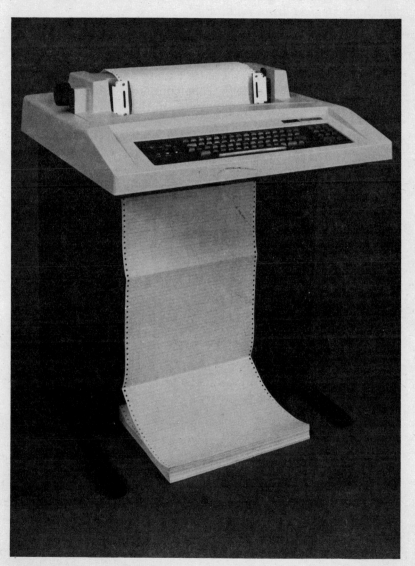

8. Line Printer (with keyboard)

that little piece of film that Hollywood spies spend lifetimes stealing from each other.

Micrographics is a field that warrants a book by itself. Consequently, we will not go into detail here. Our intent is to mention its role as a computer output device. We've already discussed printers and CRT displays. Clearly, it's not too remote a step to expect the computer output to be photographed. That's what happens in the micrographic process. One additional wrinkle is that the photograph of a single page is reduced by as much as five hundred times. As a result, micrographics computer output produces hard copy but with considerable less paper than a line printer. In addition, micrographic output devices can generate output as fast, if not faster, than hard copy line printers.

Computer output microfilm devices are called "COM devices." Output can be in the form of roll film (microfilm) or as individual photographs arranged in a grid pattern (perhaps 20 by 30) on a large piece of film (three inches by five inches); this latter output is called "microfiche." A microfilm or microfiche reader is required for human readers. The readers are basically high class magnifying glasses. One other point before we leave this type of device. Microfilm has been around for a long time and frequently brings up images of people with green eye shades in dusty rooms poring over stale records that nobody really wants. However, in recent years, the micrographics field has changed as radically as has the computer industry. As a result, in today's world micrographic is a vital information retrieval and records management tool.

Putting It All Together

We have already alluded to the similarity between a computer system and a symphony orchestra. So far we've confined our discussion to the major orchestral pieces (i.e. programming, central processor, memory, input/output). Now let's see how they all work together to produce the grand computer symphony.

The Conductor Is the Operating System

In a symphony orchestra each musician has a specific set of instructions regarding the music he or she should play. The musical instructions are written for the instrument because the symphony's composer had a vision of the many instruments working together in a musical harmony. However, in order to maintain the harmony, the orchestra must have a conductor. The conductor will ensure that each musician plays at the same speed, that the violin solo begins at the proper moment after the clarinets have played their introduction, etc.

To emphasize just how important the conductor is in the performance of an orchestra, we'll recall a story about a conflict between a famous conductor and an equally famous guest pianist. The pianist was invited to perform a concerto for a special anniversary celebration. Both the pianist and conductor considered themselves the final authority on the particular composer. However, they each had a different philosophy regarding the tempo of the music. The pianist preferred a moderate tempo, while the conductor's reputation was based on exciting rapidly paced journeys through the musical score. Naturally, the orchestra played at the conductor's pace; the pianist played at the slower pace. What happened? The orchestra came to the grand conclusion of the concerto and stopped, but the pianist was not finished, he continued at his leisurely pace for another three minutes finally arriving at his grand finale. Here was situation in which the combination of one of the world's finest conductors teamed up with one of the world's finest pianists to deliver one of the worst performances of a great concerto.

In many situations there can be only one leader. In the orchestra it is the conductor who must be in charge. Although each musician performs according to the specific set of musical notes, the conductor controls the tempo of the music, and it is the conductor who directs the different instruments as to when to start and stop, etc. From the technological point of view we can say that the conductor sets the schedules for the orchestra.

The computer's conductor is called the "operating system." The operating system is not a person, however, nor is it a piece of hardware. The operating system is a series of instructions that regulate the computer's workflow activity. Because the operating system is not a tangible piece of hardware that the customer can hold in his hand, computer manufacturers originally did not directly charge for this part of the computer system. Customers would purchase or lease specific pieces of hardware such as the processor, magnetic tape, etc. The operating system was supplied as a set of instructions recorded on a deck of punched cards or on magnetic tape. Since the actual cards or tape cost was minuscule compared to the other computer hardware, customers would certainly not understand the need to pay thousands of dollars for an operating system. Because customers were not sufficiently sophisticated to recognize the dollar value of the series of logical steps that comprised the operating system, the manufacturer furnished the operating system free.

However, in many cases the computer manufacturer spent as much money in developing the operating system as in designing the rest of the system. Hundreds of man years and millions of dollars can go into the development of operating system instructions. Naturally, the manufacturer must recoup this cost. They did so by spreading the cost of operating system development over the cost of the hardware. In other words, when you purchased or leased a processor for example, a portion of the cost for this piece of hardware included a payback to the manufacturer for the operating system development costs.

With the onset of unbundling whereby the manufacturers now allow customers to purchase or lease each part separately, a number of computer systems feature the operating system as part of their price lists. The customer now has the option of purchasing only the hardware from the manufacturer while obtaining the operating system from a "third party independent" who specialized in selling programming and operating system software directly to the computer user. While third party software vendors offer price discounts, these special operating systems are only available for a selected number of computer models and only sophisticated users will take a chance on them.

The operating system is responsible for a variety of control functions. It establishes priorities so that if two terminals want to input data at the same time, the operating system will decide which one should enter the data first. In addition, the operating system will remember that the second terminal is waiting. If while the second terminal is waiting, a third more important terminal wants to gain access, the operating system will continue to delay the second terminal. But how long can the second terminal wait?

The operating system does not have a mind of its own. Remember, it's only a series of programmed instructions (although an extremely lengthy and complicated set of instructions). Just as with any other program, the human designer of the operating system must plan for all contingencies in advance and provide rules as well as procedures to follow when they occur. Because, a typical computer system must handle several input/output devices, various auxiliary and main memory accesses, and general internal housekeeping, it is not surprising that operating systems are complicated and require large programming staffs for their creation.

Another thing to bear in mind is that when the operating system is performing, it is using the same processor as all the other computer programs. Each instruction must go through the various registers we discussed in the chapter on the central processor. So while the operating system is establishing priorities, giving computer efficiency utilization reports, etc., the payroll application is not being performed. The operating system is an overhead function, it does not produce any of the actual work that is the reason for obtaining a computer in the first place. In fact, it is not a rare occurrence for the operating system overhead to consume up to eighty or ninety percent of the computer's processing time. While this may seem wasteful, remember that everything within the computer happens so quickly that there's plenty of time to spare. However, as users become more sophisticated and introduce more applications they are also becoming dissatisfied with the operating system overhead costs. But just as the orchestra's conductor has his own dressing room and receives a considerably larger salary than any of the individual musicians, so the operating system charges for its services in a different currency.

In addition to establishing priorities and serving as the computer system's traffic policemen, the operating system is also the internal auditor. So much is happening so quickly within the computer. The operating system produces special reports that indicate how efficiently the system is performing. Are certain devices waiting too long to gain access to the central processor? Is data efficiently stored in memory or are there large gaps of empty memory areas, or should the operator replace a particular magnetic tape reel now or at a later time, etc.? These are some questions that an examination of operating system efficiency reports can help to answer.

Loading the System

We have been emphasizing that the computer system itself is simply a collection of brainless electronic components and that the programming software gives the system its direction. Since the hardware and software are manufactured independently, how do they get together? In other words, how does the software become loaded into the hardware?

When the computer first arrives, the processor's main memory is blank, while the operating system and other software is provided in the form of a magnetic tape, magnetic disk, deck of punched cards, punched paper tape, etc. The software is recorded at the factory on these machine readable media. As a result, all that is required is to have the processor read information from the appropriate medium. However, since the processor has no instructions, how will this be accomplished?

In addition to the major software, the computer arrives with a "bootstrap loader." This is a special program consisting of about twenty instructions that can be manually inserted into the computer. The processor contains a series of buttons and switches that can send signals to its main memory. The human operator changes the switch settings and pushes the appropriate buttons in accordance with the directions provided with the bootstrap loader program. Once the bootstrap is loaded, the computer can then automatically receive additional programs that will in turn control the loading of other programs until all the required programs are loaded. As you can see, the complete process is one for which the computer loads itself by literally "pulling itself up by its bootstraps."

Once the bootstrap program is loaded, the remainder of the other "utility" programs can be introduced. These utility programs don't perform any application. Rather they control the operation of the various input/output and auxiliary storage devices. For example, the operating instructions for a CRT display are different from those of the high speed line printer. So there will be a separate utility program for each device. We must emphasize that the user does not write utility programs; the manufacturer provides them.

After the utility programs are loaded, the operating system can be loaded from its medium. Here again, the manufacturer will provide the operating system as sets of instructions on a magnetic tape reel, magnetic disk pack, etc. Since the utility programs have already been loaded, the operating system instructions can be read into the processor memory from the device that is appropriate for its medium (i.e. if on magnetic tape reel then it uses a magnetic tape drive as the input device).

Will the Cup Runneth Over?

Up to this point, the processor's main memory has been loaded with the bootstrap loader, the utility programs, and the operating system. As yet, we have not loaded any programs for performing applications (the real work such as payroll, inventory control, etc., the reason for obtaining the computer system in the first place). To simplify terminology we will refer to the non-application programs as "overhead" or "housekeeping" software.

Not only is the overhead software located in main memory, but it occupies from fifty to seventy percent of the available memory. Don't be shocked; remember, we discussed the formidable requirements of the operating system software, what it must do, and also how a large number of instructions are required for its implementation. However, things are not as bleak as they might first appear. Generally, the average computer installation does not process all of its applications at the same time; accounts payable can be performed, then accounts receivable, then payroll (we'll talk about simultaneous applications processing later). So the twenty-five to fifty percent of main memory not occupied by the overhead software is available for the application programs, one at a time. Indeed, it's for this very reason that the system needs auxiliary storage.

Let us consider how the three applications (payables, receiveable, payroll) might be performed on a system that has 32 Kbytes main memory capacity, but the overhead software occupies 24 Kbytes of the main memory.

Each application along with its data can reside on a magnetic tape that is stored on a shelf. When one of the applications is scheduled to be processed, the tape is placed on a magnetic tape reader that transfers the program and its data into the computer's main memory. Once the application is comfortably situated in main memory, the computer performs the application, updates the data, and writes the updated information back onto the magnetic tape. The tape is removed and placed back on the shelf until the next time the application will be processed.

Some applications are performed several times a day. As a result, continually loading and unloading magnetic tape reels can be wearing. One approach to alleviate this procedure is to have the application reside on a desk pack which is housed in a disk drive connected to the processor. (This is called an on-line disk drive.) Whenever the application is ready to be processed, the operating system calls for the data from the disk drive. In this operation, the disk's moving arm will travel to the area on the particular surface that holds the program. When the arm reaches the beginning of the data area, the information will be read and transferred into main memory. The processor will perform the application and upon completion the data will be transferred back to the disk.

Clearly, more than one application can reside on the same disk pack. The only restriction is that the disk pack has sufficient storage capacity. At this point we can't say whether all applications should reside on disk, or on tape, or what the proper combination should be. This is strictly dependent on the nature of the applications at each computer installation. We do, however, wish to point out that you should strike some sort of balance between the applications that will be off-line and those that will reside on-line. As in all tradeoffs its a balance between speed and cost.

Now, in the situation we are discussing, only 8 Kbytes

of main memory are available for applications software. Clearly, if any of the application programs need more than 8 Kbytes, there will be a problem. However, it's not insurmountable. Here's a number of options that the user can explore.

• Most computer systems offer a range of main memory capacities for each model. If the model in this example has a maximum main memory capacity of 64 Kbytes, then the user can obtain up to 32 Kbytes of additional main memory. The memory can be obtained from the computer manufacturer or from third party independents who specialize in offering memory upgrades. However, what if the processor model in this example has already reached its maximum main memory capacity? The user cannot obtain additional memory; it won't fit. The only way to expand memory capacity would be to replace the computer with a larger model computer system. This can be an expensive and time consuming effort, so we'll explore other alternatives. However, as an aside, we do wish to note that it is usually a good idea to avoid obtaining a computer system at maximum memory capacity. Plan for expansion by getting a model that enables you to perform your work with a main memory size that is in the mid range of the maximum capacity.

• If the main memory cannot be expanded, another alternative is to reduce the overhead software, thereby freeing up some of the main memory. Some portions of the operating system and utilities can reside on disk. When they are needed, the remaining portion of the operating system can transfer just those portions into main memory. This approach is feasible, but it does slow down the system since processing cycles (time) will be used up in swapping data between main memory and disk. Another approach is to have more efficiently written overhead software so that it has less instructions and occupies less main memory space. Third party software vendors are beginning to offer such alternatives to manufacturer supplied overhead software, but this approach should not be attempted by unsophisticated users because overhead software is so complex that such major changes can lead to unforseen complications.

• Still another approach is to reduce the size of the application programs. This can be achieved by writing more efficient programs that require less instructions to implement the same logic. A thriving third party software business has developed in an attempt to satisfy the need for more efficiently written applications programs. Since an applications program is not nearly as complicated as the operating system, many users have successfully resolved the problem of insufficient main memory by taking this route.

Again we must emphasize that the approach to be followed by any particular computer installation is entirely dependent upon the nature of the specific installation. There is no single correct approach. It requires an understanding of your needs in the light of your specific operations. However, you can arrive at the best solution if you are aware of the various options available.

Programming Languages and Compilers

While we could have discussed the subject of programming languages and compilers in the chapter on Programming, we feel you'll get a better understanding of these often misunderstood subjects at this point in the text since by now you are somewhat more at home with the world of the computer.

In the chapter on Programming, we introduced the concept of subroutines and how they are used to simplify writing programs. They consist of a set of instructions that are frequently used by the main program.

In an extreme case, one can consider that a complete program is itself a subroutine. Take for example the telephone dialing program we have discussed. If one were to write a program for operating a company that sold magazines over the telephone, one procedure that would require repeated implementation would be the telephone dialing routine. If this procedure were part of an overall system of instructions, it's clear that we could label the routine by the name DIAL and treat it as a subroutine within the framework of the main program.

If all the people involved in dialing telephone numbers held a meeting and agreed to call that same routine DIAL by the same name, then that particular routine can be used by everyone without change. Stretching terminology somewhat (for the sake of clarity) we can even say that the term DIAL is a word in the "language" of those people involved in telephoning, but this is not so strange. The word "television" is in our language today, but it did not exist in the last century. When we say "television" we immediately bring to mind a picture tube, electronic circuits, entertainment, and a variety of other elements that are the components of the subroutine "television."

Each of us is a consumer, so the words "dial" and "television" are part of our language. But terms like "square root" and "exponent" are not as commonly used by the average layperson. These words then are more a part of the language of mathematics and science. On the other hand, words like "sort," "merge" and "files," are terms frequently used in a business environment for processing records. As a result, they are part of the language of business today.

We could continue with additional examples to point out words that are important in the language of the architect, artist, poet, soldier, etc. A poet can decipher the meaning of one of the mathematician's words by referring to the dictionary. There he'll find a series of words that explain the meaning of the searched for word. The definition is in a sense a subroutine for explaining the word. We might say that the dictionary is a storehouse of "word subroutines."

Bookstores sell dictionaries of mathematics, of science, of business, etc. They're specialized dictionaries intended for use in specific applications. By limiting definitions to specific subject areas, these dictionaries are easier to use and occupy less paper storage. Computer people have through the years developed "dictionaries" and "languages" for specialized professional activities. The two most common are Fortran and Cobol.

Fortran is a computer language designed to be used by scientists and mathematicians. It stands for *FOR*mula *TRAN*slator.

Cobol is a language developed for use in the business environment. It stands for *CO*mmon *B*usiness *O*riented *L*anguage.

We speak of Fortram and Cobol as "programming languages." Basically, they each consist of a set of words. Each word is itself a subroutine. The programmer does not have to be concerned about the defining subroutine. He can write his programs using the Fortran words or Cobol words, just as an author who uses English words to write a book doesn't include in his writing the definitions of the words he uses.

We humans know the definition of a great many words. This knowledge comes from learning vocabulary in school so that the definitions are stored in a dictionary in our minds. However, there are many words whose definitions we do not remember and never knew in the first place. To learn the meaning of these words, we refer to a dictionary consisting of printed words on a paper sheet. Whether we "remember" the definition or not, we are still referring to a dictionary.

By now you should realize that the computer's highest capability is at its very best far below the human's for things of the mind. So if we humans require a dictionary to understand the meaning of words, it is not very surprising that the computer needs Fortran and Cobol dictionaries to understand their respective words. However, in the case of computers they're not called dictionaries. Computer people use the term "compilers" when referring to computer language dictionaries.

A compiler is a group of subroutines. Each word in the programming language is defined by a series of instructions that make up that word's subroutine. The Fortran programming language uses a Fortran compiler. The Cobol programming language uses a Cobol compiler.

When a compiler is operating it is implementing the defining subroutines. Since, in the strict sense, a compiler does not really perform applications programming (e.g. payroll), we place compiler activity in the software overhead category alongside of operating systems and utilities.

Compiling

The process of translating a Fortran or Cobol statement into its subroutines is called "compiling" or (perhaps more grammatically correct) "compilation." Here's how the process works.

Most manufacturers furnish Fortran and Cobol compilers with their computer systems. The compiler is a software routine that translates the programming language statements into its individual instructions. We say that the compiler translates from the higher level programming to the lower level "machine language."

A compiler can occupy considerable storage space. Some are more efficient translators than others. This also applies to the more familiar word "dictionarys." Some are large and oversized containing verbose definitions of many words we hardly ever use, while others are skimpy editions that provide little real information. However, to the credit of both dictionary and compiler authors, most fall between these extremes.

Usually, the compiler will reside in main memory. As a result, it too takes up storage space that would otherwise be used by applications programs. Let us consider that we want to process a payroll program written in Cobol. We inform the operating system that we'll need the payroll program from the appropriate disk storage and that the program is written in Cobol. The operating system will then schedule the Cobol compiler program.

Each Cobol instruction from the payroll program will be analyzed by the compiler program and decomposed into its subroutine instructions. The subroutine instructions are stored temporarily until the complete payroll program is decomposed. When this is accomplished, a completely translated payroll program is available for processing.

Note that the first phase of this activity was the compilation process. Clearly compilation uses processor cycles and, as a result, while compilation is taking place, other programs are not processing. After the payroll program is processed, the user can erase the translated program stored in main memory in order to free it up for other programs. However, if the program will be used again, another approach is to make a copy of the compiled program on the disk. The next time the program will be run, the compilation process can be avoided since the machine language program is already on disk.

You may question why we should store a compiled program if we have a compiler to perform the translating. Yes, the compilation takes time, but we knew that in advance. If we wanted to save the compilation time why did we not write the program in the lower level language to begin with. Why did we write the payroll program in Cobol in the first place? We wrote the program in Cobol because it is much easier for humans to program in higher level languages. So we save the human's time by creating the program in the higher level language and then save the computer's time by leaving the program in the lower level language after it is translated.

However, whether a program is compiled each time it is used, or whether it is compiled once and then copied in its lower level form is another one of those factors that really depends on the nature of the specific computer installation.

One other example, we said that the compiler usually resides in main memory. However, in many installations both Fortran and Cobol programs are run. This would require storing two compilers in main memory. If three or four different programming languages were run, main memory would have to accommodate a corresponding number of compilers. In such a situation, we could run out of main memory. As a result, for such cases, the compiler programs are stored on disk and when for example, a Cobol program is run, the Cobol compiler is transferred from disk to main memory, then (for example) the payroll program is transferred, and then the compilation process takes place. Here you can see that additional overhead is added to the system. Is it any wonder that overhead processing occupies most of the computer's processing cycles with comparatively little going into useful applications processing?

The Dynamic Computer

Again let us consider some examples of the different ways that computer processing can be performed and what is involved in each.

Batch Processing. Batch processing is the oldest form

of computing and originates its name from the fact that all jobs to be processed are held in individual batches awaiting their turn. Consider a company with a single computer center that handles payroll, receivables, and payables. Each job will be processed separately according to a predetermined schedule.

The payroll department, for example, will send the necessary information regarding the number of hours worked, hourly salaries, fringe benefits, etc. This information can be on special printed forms or in whatever fashion consistent with the operation of the company. However, the data must be transcribed into machine readable form. One way to accomplish this is to transfer the information to punched cards. After this is done, there will exist a stack of punched cards. A number of these stacks constitute a "batch." Today, most people are avoiding the punched cards and instead transferring the information to magnetic tape and disk media also called batches (a holdover from the old days).

The computer operator goes through the batch, taking each job according to some priority. Sometimes it can be on a first come first served basis, other times if it's a job for the company president, it might take precedence over the others.

Once a job is selected, the operator reads its specifications; which input/output devices will it require, will it use the Cobol compiler, etc.?

The operator loads the card deck (or magnetic tape) on the card reader (or magnetic tape drive) and the data is read and stored in main memory. Next the program that will manipulate the data is transferred from the disk to main memory (assuming that it does not already reside there). The program will be compiled, then it will process the inputted data. After processing, output will be produced in the form of printed reports, punched cards, magnetic tapes or whatever form found useful for that particular application. The computer operator will remove the output and place it in a special location where the user will pick up the processing results or wait for the mail system to make delivery.

In batch processing, the person who requires the information does not get involved in the actual running of the computer; it is left to the computer operator. The user may wait several hours for the results or several days. Sometimes this is not a problem, other times the delay can seem interminable. But that is only one problem with batch processing. If the data or program contains an error that prevents the computer from processing, the job is aborted. In most computer installations the operator will send the aborted job back to the user who must make the correction. Then the process begins all over again with the job taking its place in the end of the line. Yes, the user can speak with the computer center manager to get a higher priority for the aborted job. But what if this is the fifth time the job was aborted? What if other users are also requesting higher priorities for their aborted jobs? What about the regular users who are waiting, what if . . . ? As you can see batch processing can lead to many problems and in some cases quarrels if it is not properly controlled. However, as with everything else involving groups of people, if it is properly scheduled and users follow properly delineated procedures it can be very effective and efficient. Indeed, most computer installations are engaged in batch processing, so it can't be all that difficult.

Real Time Processing

Real time processing does not imply that batch processing is fake time. The point here is that with real time processing the user is getting results immediately and he is also interacting with the computer in a conversational manner.

For real time or interactive processing, the user sits at an input device that provides human input and human readable output. The most popular type is a CRT terminal that has a keyboard for entry and a display screen for output. The user keys in the data and instructions, and the computer answers back by sending messages on the screen.

In the most elementary fashion, the user can key in each instruction of his program by means of the keyboard. However, if we're dealing with a large program of perhaps one thousand instructions, this can be a tedious process. So the best approach is to load the program onto a magnetic disk or tape that's on-line to the processor. (Of course for smaller programs the operator can use the keyboard for entering the program.)

Now it is important to note that the user's interaction with the computer is not magical. The computer's operating system was designed to operate in this manner. Manufacturers design operating systems to handle the housekeeping for real time interactive computing.

If we're still talking about the payroll problem, the user will hit appropriate keys to inform the system that he's performing payroll. The operating system will cause the payroll program to transfer from the disk to main memory. Then the program will be compiled (if necessary). Now the operating system will cause a message to be flashed on the screen. While specific messages will depend on the particular system, one example would be "program loaded, enter employee names." After each name is entered, the system might flash a message "enter hours worked."

In this type of system, the programmer can provide built in error detection capabilities so that errors are detected and corrected on the spot. For example, the number of hours worked could be a number less than sixty (company policy is to pay for a regular forty-hour week with a maximum of twenty hours overtime). If in keying the number of hours worked, the operator mistakenly enters an alphabetic letter or a number greater than sixty, the system will flash an error message on the screen informing the user that the data is incorrect. The error can then be corrected immediately.

If company policy changes at some time so that fifty hours becomes the maximum, the operator can make a change to the program from the terminal. In a sense the operator is conversing with the computer and it is all happening in the here and now (real time).

After all the data is inputted, the operator can read the answers as they are displayed on the screen. Other output alternatives are also available. If a typewriter terminal were used instead of a CRT, then the output would be typed on paper. The best of both worlds could be achieved by using a combined typewriter/CRT terminal. If the output will consist of thousands of lines, then the typewriter terminal may be too slow, in which case, the processor can be instructed to send the output to a high speed line printer. Output can be on all of these devices as well as on magnetic tape if that would fill the bill.

The main point to stress in discussing real time computing is that the user interacts with the computer and gets essentially immediate responses.

Time Sharing

From the computer's point of view, one person sitting at a terminal performing interactive processing can be quite inefficient. During the time that the human keys in one character, the processor can be going through a thousand cycles. However, if the processor is waiting for the information contained in that single keystroke, then the thousand cycles are wasted.

The thousand cycles can be used, however, by employing a time sharing operating system. With time sharing, multiple terminals (in some cases as many as fifty) can be hooked up to the computer at the same time. The operating system allocates "time slices" to each terminal (perhaps a few thousandths of a second to each terminal). The time slices are given in a round robin fashion to each terminal; things are happening very fast. So fast in fact, that the human at the terminal doesn't even sense that he's not attached to the computer during those milisecond intervals. The process can be compared to a high speed revolving circular switch.

During each time slice, the computer performs the processing for the terminal that is connected. The details of keeping track of everyone's programs and storage devices are not simple, but from the user's point of view he thinks that he has the complete system to himself. Consequently, from any single user's point of view he is engaged in interactive real time processing. However, since many terminals are active at the same time, the user pool can more effectively utilize the computer's resources.

Many companies offer commercial time sharing services to the general business community. These services enable a user whose workload does not warrant the expense of an in-house system to purchase computer capability when he needs it and for just the right level of computing needed. In many companies where the workload of individual users does not warrant their own interactive computing capability, various departments can pool their money to install a time sharing system for use within the company.

7

Crime and Personal Computer Controls

One major new area of the contemporary scene that has arrived with the computer is "computer crime." The newspapers frequently feature stories describing major embezzlements, defalcations, and other scams that net the perpetrators hundreds of thousands of dollars.

In a particularly fascinating caper, the consultant to a bank's computer processing center diverted ten million dollars to a Swiss bank by breaking the computerized money transfer code. He then invested the money in diamonds and, when he was caught several months later, the diamonds had increased in value by about two million dollars. While the bank subsequently regained its funds (in fact the bank came out ahead since it was the beneficiary of the smart diamond investment), and the criminal was caught, in many other cases, businesses have been ruined by inadequately controlled computer systems.

While crime and criminals make interesting and exciting

copy, it turns out that most computer problems arise from honest people making human errors. It is surprising that most businesses tend to disregard established controls on bookkeepers, suppliers, and other financially related individuals when a new computer is programmed to take care of the tedious work.

The owner of a small variety store having perhaps twenty employees and four cash registers will carefully scrutinize the journal tapes produced by his "manual" cash registers; he will review each bill received from outside vendors and carefully count each item to guarantee the accuracy of inventory. While a good computer will make each of these tasks simpler to perform (and will perhaps be more accurate as well), the computer does not relieve the businessman of the need to continue careful scrutiny. Promotional literature boastfully promises a variety of benefits from the use of a particular computer. Unfortunately, the benefits only occur if everything else goes according to plan. But in computer applications, as in all of life situations, most things don't always go according to plan, and the truly important decisions are those reserved for cases where the process diverges from the plan. The underlying danger presented by the use of a computer is a false sense of security.

A viable defense against human error also serves as a useful deterrent to the consequences of computer crimes. While the crime may not be prevented (just as human error happens unexpectedly), its impact can be minimized by implementing proper controls. Drawing on the wisdom of several old clichés such as "pencils have erasers because people make mistakes" and "jet planes have two engines in case one fails," we must assume that errors will occur and crimes will be attempted. The important thing to remember, however, is that with proper awareness and controls these problems can be kept to a minimum.

Since personal computers are used in a nonstructured environment, the possibility for error can be even greater. While home applications may not be as significant as in business situations (e.g., home budgeting compared to inventory control) the personal computer is certainly important to the individual who must complete his or her income tax statement. Consequently, if all the tax information (such as wages earned, records of deductions, etc.) is stored only on a diskette or cassette, what will happen if the storage medium is lost or inadvertently erased? When the task was done manually, the individual probably maintained duplicate records and paid special attention to the more important documents. Because of the computer's ability to make the process "paperless," the same individual may overlook various controls that should be present. Why? Because a false sense of security frequently lulls people into assuming the computer is "taking care of it."

Controls (Preventive, Detective, Corrective)

Naturally, it is best if all activity is performed to perfection. However, as the poet Alexander Pope said: "To err is human . . ." In a reasonable world we must assume some errors will occur and prepare for them by establishing controls. These controls can be preventive, detective, corrective, or some combination of the three.

Take the case of a safe deposit box in a home. Clearly the box will be hidden from view and locked in order to *prevent* unauthorized access to the contents. (Unauthorized access can range from burgling to inadvertently opening the box and spilling its contents.) If access to the box is gained, hopefully an alarm will go off, signifying the unauthorized access was *detected*. Finally, if a policeman is nearby and arrests the burglar, the contents will be replaced and the theft will be *corrected*.

Preventive Controls

As the name implies, these controls are used to prevent errors from happening in the first place. Before instituting preventive controls in a business application, however, one must balance the cost of these controls against the risk of an error occurring and the cost of that error to the organization. For example, one control that prevents an unauthorized individual from accessing an inventory file that is present on a computer is a password.

Before a program can be utilized, an operator must enter a suitable response to the computer's request for proper identification. In many cases there are several levels of password access; one password allows an operator to scan and view the contents of the file while another password allows him or her to make changes to it.

If there are too many levels of password access required, the efficiency of the operation will diminish. It may take longer to access the file than to do the actual work. Additionally, if an operator must remember too many passwords, he or she may resort to writing them down. Unauthorized individuals could discover the passwords and their original purpose would be defeated. Finally, an employer must consider how a temporary worker can gain access to the file in order for business to proceed.

Each of the above considerations of cost and efficiency loss must be weighed against the benefits of preventive controls. The cost of a preventive control may be so prohibitive the best decision may be to allow errors to happen but to institute good detective controls so that when errors do occur, immediate corrective action can be taken. This kind of decision would be wise in cases where the chances of an error occurring are quite small. Why put in a ten-thousand-dollar alarm system if you only have several hundred dollars' worth of goods to protect?

Detective Controls

Since few things go according to plan, we must expect that, from time to time, preventive controls will fail and various established procedures may be violated. These failures need not be catastrophic if they are detected so that proper action can be taken. If a thief overrides the preventive controls of a locked safe deposit box in a bank (e.g., locked doors, guarded patrols, etc.) an alarm will go off to notify all concerned that entry has occurred.

A familiar type of detective control is the fire alarm or smoke detector. A smoke detector sounding an alarm in the middle of the night can alert and save the lives of a sleeping family.

A red light is a popular detective control among manufacturers of electronic components. Many personal computers are equipped with indicators that display or flash red as a warning for operators to pause before proceeding because some control has been inadvertently overridden. In other cases, the software itself includes detective controls that cause audible alarms to be sounded by the computer and its various components. A blown fuse is another detective control; when the whole system shuts down, an operator becomes alerted to the fact that there has been an excessive surge of electrical power.

Corrective Controls

Once the preventive control has been circumvented and the detective control has indicated that a problem has occurred, it becomes necessary to correct the damage or to, at least, limit its impact.

For example, while a smoke detector or fire alarm alerts people to a fire, it might also bring about corrective action immediately by causing a sprinkler system to shower water over the premises. The corrective control is intended to keep the damage within reasonable bounds.

A business that keeps only one list of its customers' names, addresses, and accounts receivable on tape or disk may have a short lifespan because it will always be vulnerable to the list's disappearance or destruction. When that happens the business has no record of its customers and an inability to collect funds owed. Clearly, such lists should be duplicated (called back-up files) and stored off-premises so that they can be reconstructed if necessary.

Input Controls

Input controls are among the most important in the computer process. The familiar term "GIGO" (Garbage In Garbage Out) is equally applicable to both personal and business computers. For examples of input controls, we will consider the workflow for order processing and bill paying in a small business, which accepts telephone orders for automobile tires. An employee on the business site records the information and then enters the order into a computer via a terminal. Let us see what kind of controls are needed and why.

The first question to consider is whether the calling party is authorized to place the order. One would assume that the owner of a garage (if that is the nature of the firm requesting the tires) would place the order if it involves considerable money. It may be that the owner's voice is recognized by the dispatcher at the other end, but in a large organization this would not be a reliable indicator. One solution (already mentioned previously) would be the use of passwords. In order for the garage owner to allow several of his employees to place orders, and at the same time to control the financial impact of each, he could arrange for several passwords so that one employee could order for up to one thousand dollars, another for up to two thousand, and so on. Having received the correct password, the dispatcher could assume that the caller is authorized.

When the order is received, the dispatcher must determine if he is obtaining the correct information. Since nothing is in writing at this point, one possible approach is for the dispatcher to repeat each statement of the order to the individual at the other end. Obviously, a more accurate procedure, which would include stronger error-preventing controls, would be a written document sent by the garage owner to the tire dealer. But this would cause a time delay and prevent the garage from receiving its tires immediately. A "looser" verbal control is chosen over the strict control of a written order to hasten the transaction.

Now let us focus on the dispatcher who will enter the information into the computer. The information from the customer must be recorded in a readable and organized manner. This is a frequently overlooked aspect of computer data entry. In this situation we might assume that paper is not significant since it involves a computer transaction. But if the dispatcher wrote the order on the back of a cigarette package rather than on a well-designed form, it would probably not be an accurate entry. Of course, the last statement is somewhat extreme, but good form design is one of the most important, yet most neglected, areas of business activity. If the data are recorded on good forms, the dispatcher can record several orders, stack them, and later perform the data entry function in a continuous and smooth flow. If he is interrupted during this process, he can easily identify where he left off and continue at the proper place.

As the data are read and fed into the computer by means of a keyboard device, the dispatcher must insure that he has avoided typographical errors. After typing a manuscript, it is a generally accepted practice to proofread the final manuscript against the source document. If any errors are detected, a notation is made and the information is retyped. Such a simple procedure in the case of computer data entry would save many headaches.

Surprisingly the precaution of checking a hard-copy print-out is more often avoided than followed. A visit to the various computer stores will demonstrate that most systems are sold with CRT visual screens instead of hard-copy printers as output devices. Frequently, users try to save money by eliminating the hard-copy printer. Such a savings is often worthwhile, as in the case where the hobbyist is primarily interested in game activities. However, when deciding on the type of output device to use for your system, remember that checking what you have input to the computer against a hard-copy printout is a far superior control than checking your input against what appears on the CRT screen.

For data entry, the computer can provide several forms of control by utilizing its built-in logic. For example, "range restrictions" can be set so that payment to a certain vendor is under a fixed amount. If an operator incorrectly enters a higher amount, the computer will set off an alarm, a bell, or simply lock the keyboard to notify the individual that such an error has occurred.

Many personal computers do not have the sophistication of larger systems that include the various range-checking features. But as a result of these comments, you should not throw out your personal or hobby computer and replace it with a more expensive system that will have better input controls. Determine whether your particular applications require stronger controls. Frequently, they do not. However, as you expand the applications of your personal computer, you may require better input controls. While specific cross-over points cannot be given here (because each situation is unique), you must always reevaluate your needs and be ready to upgrade to a new level of control.

Software Controls

Control over software integrity is a difficult task to accomplish, but the user of any computer program should always be aware that in some cases "what you see may not be what you get." Even for cases in which you are able to explain to the programmer exactly what you need (or if you write the program yourself), unauthorized changes can occur. It is important to introduce a procedure to prevent the changes from occurring and to detect them if they do.

What are some of the problems that can happen if software is improperly changed? Consider the simple case where a program originally intends to add two numbers, but an inadvertent change now makes the program multiply the two numbers. This can be a severe problem if you are calculating the amount of money you should pay to your vendors. Whereas last month you sent a fifteen-dollar check (nine plus six), this month, with the new multiplicative program change, the check is for fifty-four dollars (nine times six).

In a sense, when a software change occurs, the rules of the system have been changed and various processes can go haywire. Changes can occur intentionally or by accident. The most well-known types of unauthorized intentional changes are those made for fraudulent purposes. For example, if Mr. Bad is the recipient of the monthly checks discussed above, then he will certainly profit from the multiplication change. On the other hand, intentional changes can be made in all honesty, but a typographical error was made (instead of entering a plus sign the operator entered a multiplication sign). Ideally, the operator should have followed the procedure outlined in the Input Controls section where we discussed the need for proofing against a hard-copy printout, but life does not always follow the pages of books.

Since computer software specifies rules for implementing ongoing processes and activities, and these systems themselves change, it is only natural that software undergoes continous changes and modifications. Recognizing this, we must implement appropriate controls to insure that accurate processing is maintained.

The major preventive control is to allow only authorized individuals to have access to the software. This is accomplished by using passwords and maintaining physical control. In the latter case, all disks, diskettes, tapes, cassettes, and other removable storage media are kept in a secure environment (perhaps in a locked cabinet); and only specified individuals are allowed to handle them. Once the information on the media is loaded into the computer, it must be protected from modification by requiring certain password identification.

Assuming that all the appropriate input controls have been followed and the program changes have been accurately entered, there is still no guarantee that the computer's memory will not make some inadvertent change. While all these concerns may sound over-cautious, you must remember that software is the brain of the computer and any inconsistencies can have grave and far-reaching impact.

One interesting detective control that is more readily implemented with larger-scale computers is to have a program that adds up all the lines and/or all the characters of the program whose integrity is to be preserved. If there are any changes relative to the standard, then clearly a change has been made to the program. For example, if you add up the number of letters of the words that constitute this very page you are reading, then it is very likely that any changes (e.g., rewriting, new punctuation, etc.) will cause the reference number to change. An even more specific control would be to count the number of characters for every fifteen lines. While it may be true that the total characters per page remains constant, it would be highly probable that the reference counts within the fifteen-line segments would disagree.

The "character count" method discussed above can be expensive in the use of computer resources. It requires a separate program to do the counting, additional storage to retain the results, processor cycles to perform the calculations, and various other overhead functions. Consequently, such an approach would not be feasible for the personal or hobby computer. In fact, it is not an approach that many larger computer operations are willing to take either.

One control that can be used by personal, hobby, and larger computers and which operate economically is the "test transaction." Specifically, if the program was originally required to accept a series of numbers, perform specific algebraic/arithmetic tasks (additions, multiplications, etc.), and, after other variations, produce a predetermined result, then any variation from the expected result will indicate that a change has occurred.

Output Controls

The primary functions of output controls are to insure that only authorized individuals receive the computer's output and that it is provided in a usable format.

A mail-order house must insure that its customer mailing list is secure. If a competitor gains access to the list, the primary asset of the organization and the company itself can be lost. Proper controls would require that the company maintain an approved list of individuals who can receive copies of output reports. In addition, each individual should sign when receiving copies. If output is via display terminals such as CRTs, then passwords should certainly be used.

In the case where the output may be stock certificates, negotiable bonds, or checks, improper output controls can result in immediate and direct financial loss. As a result, limiting access to the final output is not sufficient. The output media (e.g., checks, bonds, etc.) must be maintained under tight control with access allowed only by specified computer operations personnel. Each document should be sequentially numbered and the computer program should specify which numbered documents are to be involved in the transaction.

While the computer has been a significant improvement to the information processing world, it has also provided a new ailment known as the "information glut." By virtue of its extensive processing ability, it can generate pages upon pages of data. Indeed, the important data that a user needs to perform his business functions can be buried under a pile of extraneous information. In such a case, too much information is the same as no information.

Proper format designs, whether on paper or on CRT displays, will help guard against the information glut. They allow for the data to be organized in a clear, concise, and understandable fashion. Here again, good form design turns out to be an economical and productive endeavor in the long run.

INDEX